POPE OR GOSPEL?

POPE OR GOSPEL?

DAVID SAMUEL

MARSHALLS

Marshalls Paperbacks
Marshall Morgan & Scott
1 Bath Street, London EC1V 9LB

Copyright © David Samuel 1982
First published by Marshall Morgan & Scott 1982

ISBN 0 551 00958 6

Printed in Great Britain by
Cox & Wyman Ltd., Reading

Contents

To all who are not ashamed of the Gospel of Christ

Acknowledgments
I wish to express my gratitude to my colleague Dr Derek
Scales, and to my wife, for their reading various chapters
of the typescript and offering helpful suggestions.

1: Is the Reformation over?

We live today in a religious climate in which many people consider that the differences between Rome and the Protestant churches are of very little consequence. Daily we are confronted with fresh examples of this attitude of mind. There is the feeling abroad that the Reformation has now run its course and made its point; that the Roman Catholic Church has changed and is now a very different institution from what it was at the time of the Reformation. Has not the time come, they say, for us to recognise these facts, and accept the eventual union that growing understanding and tolerance will eventually bring about?

As an article in the *Tablet*, a Roman Catholic journal, put it recently, 'When a protest movement has achieved its declared objective, should it not go into voluntary liquidation?' The Archbishop of Canterbury, at the meeting of the Anglican Consultative Council in 1981, declared that he looked forward to the eventual disappearance of the Anglican Church. Thus the Anglican and the Protestant churches generally are seen as having fulfilled their purpose in drawing attention to certain abuses in the Church of Rome. Now that those abuses, it is argued, have been removed, and Protestantism itself has changed and has been able to appreciate and absorb certain Catholic insights, the justification for the separate existence and identity of those Protestant churches has ceased. This is the mood that seems to prevail today.

The issues obscured

Because it is a mood, a feeling, a general impression people have gained, there is a strong reluctance to consider or discuss the doctrinal differences which are the real cause of division. At the same time there is a ready acceptance of assertions of agreement and unity, often in a complacent and undiscerning manner. The mood or orientation creates this predisposition to look favourably upon everything that confirms synthesis, and critically upon the suggestion that there are real and palpable differences. Why should there be this assumption that oneness is necessarily good? It is not so regarded generally in life. Monopolies are regarded today as harmful. Why should the creation of a monopoly in the Church be regarded as necessarily good? The history of the Church before the Reformation does not bear this out. There was much that was evil in that Church from which the Reformation delivered us, and for which we should be profoundly thankful. It is the irrationalism of this mood that troubles me, and the unwillingness to submit the basic presuppositions of ecumenism to any serious critical examination.

Perhaps this whole phenomenon can be expressed succinctly in an experience I had recently. I was staying in Oxford and one Sunday morning attended the University Church of St Mary's. The preacher was the Roman Catholic students' chaplain. If you had not known you would have thought he was an Anglican. There was nothing in his dress, manner or speech to suggest that he was a Roman Catholic. His sermon was uncontroversial; it was about loving God and your neighbour. He was in favour of it, as Mark Twain would have said. So you find your self asking, 'Where then is the difference?' The answer is that the difference is not seen on that kind of occasion. The differences do not surface at that level. But as I sat there I knew that on the pillar opposite the pulpit, hidden from the congregation, were the still extant marks made by the scaffolding that was erected for the trial of Archbishop Cranmer. My mind filled with another scene of the timid Cranmer making his final abjuration of the Pope and all his teachings, and the monks trying to pull him down from the scaffold. The juxtaposition of these two things seems to penetrate the religious phenomenon we experience today.

The mood, the climate in which we move is one of consensus, of synthesis and agreement. But this is only possible in the first place because ours is an unhistorical generation. In its secular isolation and complacency it does not see the 'marks of the scaffolding on the wall', or if it sees them it does not understand or appreciate what they mean. The past is regarded as so much lumber to be discarded, and in religious matters as largely an irrelevance and an embarrassment. Yet we cannot ignore it, and it will not go away simply because we wish it was not there. Christianity is itself an historical religion, ie, we believe that what happened in the past is of profound importance for today. The Christian religion is not a phenomenon of the twentieth century, though it would appear that many people would like it to be. The crises that faith has faced in the past are relevant to the present age and can save us from tragedy and folly if we have the willingness to listen.

Secondly, the present mood can only be sustained by carefully avoiding real and fundamental questions, by dealing with those matters which are non-controversial, as the Roman Catholic chaplain did. Matters which steer well clear of the doctrines that divide. But this position cannot really be maintained without a spiritually harmful effect upon the Church, for these questions are questions of truth, the truth of God's Word by which and from which the Church must live. They cannot be put into cold storage to further the interests of any movement, not even that of church unity. By what shall the Church live, and what message shall it proclaim while we are waiting for the synthesis to take place and the truth to emerge? 'Where there is no vision the people perish.' While Moses tarried on the mount the people of Israel committed fornication and idolatry. Where there is no clear, authoritative statement of the things which are to be believed, of the doctrine of the Gospel, there must be spiritual malaise and decline in the Church. And it is the nature of the Gospel which is in

11

dispute between the Roman Catholic and Protestant churches. That was what the Reformation was all about.

So the mood that prevails today is one that needs to be challenged in the name of what is true and what is good for the Church of God in this present age. If it continues to envelop the churches it can only contribute to their further decline, and stifle the clear proclamation of the Gospel.

Truth endangered

I am reminded of the student who, several years ago when all the talk in the churches was about restructuring, said to the President of the Methodist Conference, 'When the re-organisation has taken place, I suppose we shall then be able to get on with the job'. To which the President replied, 'What job?' It would appear that there are many who are saying in their hearts when the problem of Christian unity has been solved, and the one great Church has arrived, we shall then be able to proclaim the Gospel. But the question could well be, 'What Gospel?' It will then emerge that not only have the fundamental doctrines of the Gospel been put into cold storage, but dissipated in the ambiguous ecumenical formulas which are being used to obscure the plain, Scriptural doctrines that are to be found in the Confessions of the Protestant churches.

The structures of ecumenism, by which I mean the process of bargaining that goes on between the official theologians of the Roman Catholic and Protestant churches, are hostile to truth, the truth of God's Word by which the church must live. Truth is incompatible with the formal character, development and objectives of ecumenism. I see a parallel here with what Charles Davis had to say about the Roman Catholic Church in his book, *A Question of Conscience*. He argued that the structures of that church inhibited truth; that truth could not flourish in an institution, the primary purpose of which was to protect its own power and authority. Truth then becomes subservient to that end, ceases to exist in its own right, and ceases therefore to be truth. 'I find', he said, 'the spirit that subordinates truth to authority and power throughout the

12

ecclesiastical structure. I have looked in vain for a joyful sense of the value and power of truth as truth.'[1]

A similar criticism can be made of the ecumenical movement. In its commitment to visible unity, to one church (which means in concrete terms the government of a universal church by a Catholic episcopate and ultimately by a Pope) the truth is distorted and bent, as the rays of light are bent when they pass through a prism. Truth, in encountering and passing through the ecumenical process, is deflected and made to serve the end of promoting that visible unity which it is taken for granted must be the overriding consideration. It thus ceases to be truth.

If, therefore, Protestantism is drawn into this situation, in which truth is either pushed into the background because it is divisive, or wrapped in ambiguous formulas in order to produce some semblance of agreement as the basis for institutional mergers, then it will in the end be left with nothing to preach, no Gospel, no message of spiritual and saving power.

Influences at work in ecumenism

In the ecumenical movement there is an in-built bias towards the Catholic concept of the church as a visibly united body, rather than the Protestant concept of it as the company of believers ruled by the truth of God's Word revealed in Scripture. Because of this any move it takes brings it nearer to the Catholic ideal and further from the Protestant. This is seen in particular in two factors.

First, the ecumenical movement's insistence upon visible, organic unity fits in neatly with the doctrine of the Roman Catholic Church as deriving authority, ministry and grace from the historic episcopate. Once you have adopted the premise that God wills visible unity for his church you are then carried along inescapably in the direction of reunion with the historic episcopate and all the essential doctrines which adhere to that position.

Secondly, there is the matter of the highest common factor. In the terms of the Lausanne Déclaration, which formally initiated the ecumenical movement, the three

13

forms of church government, episcopal, presbyteral and congregational, are to bring their spiritual treasures together in a united church. But this means that the fundamental change has to be made by the last two. Very little alteration or adjustment is required in the episcopal churches. After such pooling of treasures the presbyteral and congregational will be found to have virtually disappeared in an episcopal church. And, of course, when the principle is extended further to a papal church, then it will mean that the papal will swallow up all three because the highest common factor must always prevail. It is built into the system. Thus the whole ecumenical movement has within it the tendency to move relentlessly in a Roman Catholic direction, to the loss of the spiritual identity and character of Protestantism.

This ecumenical discussion takes for granted that the view of episcopacy must be the Catholic one of grace transmitted through the historic episcopate. There is a Reformed understanding of episcopacy (which the Reformers of the Church of England held), which carries with it no such connotation, which subordinates episcopacy to the truth of God's Word, and does not make it essential to the being of the church. If that view prevailed there would be no constraint to move in a Catholic direction. Indeed, if that view prevailed the obsession with organic unity at the cost of truth would not have arisen in the first place.

But given the prevailing trend the whole movement must be seen to be working against the Reformation, and against the truths for which it stood. Truth is being subordinated to this powerful tendency, this dominating passion to bring the churches together in visible unity.

Toleration and indifference

The constraints which impel Protestants in a Romeward direction, at the same time compel them to sit loosely to their own doctrines, or require them to be satisfied with doctrinal formulas which are intended to assure them that some kind of agreement or understanding has been reached, and their particular 'insights' have been incorporated in the coming great Church. But this presupposes two things on the part of Protestants: 1. That they are prepared to exercise a tolerance which is indistinguishable from doctrinal indifference. And 2. That they are willing to concede that the Reformation was no more than some kind of misunderstanding about words.

First, tolerance amounting to indifference to truth. There is a true toleration to be exercised when it is recognised that the differences between two parties are so great, whether it be in matters of faith or order, that it is better for them to exist separately than to seek to continue in one body. This is toleration, not indifference to truth. There is a keen awareness of truth and it is on that basis that the parties agree to differ. Such toleration can include the willingness to consider and discuss the differences that obtain between the parties, but it recognises the futility of comprehension within one body. But today Protestants are not being asked to exercise that kind of toleration, which incidentally they themselves first devised in the form of denominations. 'Denominationalism', said Ian Henderson in his book *Power without Glory*, 'is the conviction that, if you cannot agree with your fellow Christians, it is better to live with them than to kill them', as had happened in the Middle Ages. 'Denominationalism is a valuable device that enables you honestly and openly to disagree with your fellow Christian on what for them are fundamentals, but for you are overbeliefs, and vice versa.'[2]

But the ecumenical movement is not asking us to exercise toleration of this kind, for it is an attack on denominationalism. Rather in the name of unity and reconciliation, or as some would see it, the merging of denominations, it is asking us to exercise a toleration that admits even doctrinal contradictions in the same body, to accept unity on the basis of the Catholic conception of the nature of the Church as a hierarchically organised body (in the full priestly sense of the term) and not to insist for the time being upon those doctrines of Protestantism which conflict with this understanding. But this is not toleration; it is indifference to truth, and such indifference can only in the course of time create a spiritual desert.

On the face of it, it would appear to be a demand which no self-respecting Protestant could meet, but it is being advanced because many of the Protestant churches and their leaders are more than half-way there. Already they have left the Reformation far behind and are guided not by doctrine but by pragmatism. Moreover, our age is one which makes superficial judgements about religion. It does not live by every word that proceeds out of the mouth of God, but lives out of and from the material bread of the world. Religion is almost an alien phenomenon in the life of the secular world and the largely secularized churches. The important issues of truth which arise from the Word of God, and once actuated men to live and die for them (a climate of thought and conviction in which indifference would have seemed impossible), do not impinge upon the conscience of the present age. It is difficult, they say, with regard to the Reformation, to see what the fuss was all about. But the fault lies not with the Reformers, but with ourselves; it is not that the Word of God is not alive, but the present age is spiritually dead. Because the spiritual myopia of the present generation renders these things indistinct, does not in fact make them unreal. On the contrary they are the only real issues of religion. The truths of God's Word can be recognised by those for whom it is life, but the spiritually dead are indifferent to everything.

Thus, appealing to Protestantism to be indifferent to its own reality and truth which arise from the Word of God is not a difficult matter in the present moribund state of its institutional churches. The present trend towards ecumenical absorption with the Church of Rome is only possible because of such indifference.

The Church of Rome knows this. It sees that everything is moving its way, that there is an in-built bias in ecumenism, which together with the spiritual deadness and doctrinal indifference that prevails in Protestantism must carry things towards the conception of organic unity that is integral to the Roman system. All it has to do is keep a low profile, avoid divisive issues, and present its own position in the most favourable light.

The other thing expected of Protestants is that they should come to regard the Reformation as largely a dispute about words. It is conceded that there were abuses in the Church at the time which aggravated the misunderstanding, but when these abuses had been dealt with it is said that the difference between the parties was really little more than a matter of emphasis upon one aspect of truth rather than another. The resolution of the difference is therefore possible now in the new atmosphere of goodwill and understanding, and with the clearer insight that has been attained into the historical circumstances of the Reformation.

This reading of the problem is unsatisfactory for several reasons. It is in the first place far too superficial an assessment of a profound movement of thought and religious feeling which has had an abiding effect upon the history of Europe and the world. It cannot be dismissed in this way. Such movements do not arise from mere misunderstandings. Men do not usually die for semantics. Religions are not founded upon verbal quibbles. We might as well explain the origin of Christianity in the same way. The difference between Christ and the Pharisees might be explained thus, and of course there are those who are ready to advance such a hypothesis, but it carries no weight. There is no reason why it should do so in the case of the Reformation either.

In the second place a mere difference about words would not have escaped the notice of those engaged in the controversy. Those who are familiar with the conferences and debates of the Reformation period know how very thoroughly the ground was gone over. Even attempts to reconcile the parties by inventing ambiguous formulas were resorted to, a device which is sometimes regarded as a novelty of ecumenical dialogue. Had it been a mere logomachy it would have come to light in the exhaustive discussions of that period.

As for the argument that the historical circumstances rather than the religious issues drove the parties apart, and that greater historical research into these circumstances, eg, the forces at work behind the Council of Trent, the preponderance of Italian bishops, etc., will bring them together again, this seems to me to be a two-edged weapon in the hands of those who wield it. We ourselves are also historically conditioned, and it can therefore be argued that from our position in the twentieth century we do not appreciate, or treat this subject with the seriousness it deserves, nor recognise the central place these questions had, and should still have today, in men's lives.

Our age is one which trivializes spiritual issues, which steers clear of deep commitment and of any sense of moral absolutes or transcendence. How can we set out to judge the depth and importance of the doctrinal questions of the Reformation? By discounting their importance and giving greater weight to the historical circumstances we reveal ourselves for what we are—the children of a secular age. We judge ourselves rather than them. The only proper conclusion to which we can come is, that an age such as theirs, an age of faith and spiritual awareness, rightly judged the issues that really mattered, and that an age of spiritual decline and weakness, such as ours, is more likely to be wrong on such questions. We should have the humility to learn from an age of spiritual revival and religious faith.

The Reformation is not over, nor is it dead. It is only buried under the rubbish of the present age. It has been lost sight of in the spiritual myopia of the present century. It is due to be rediscovered at any moment, and its rediscovery will bring a new awareness of true and vital religion.

2: What is Protestantism?

The Protestant Reformation was essentially a religious movement, concerned with Biblical doctrine, though many other factors were involved. The new learning and culture brought to light by the Renaissance, which contributed to a fresh appreciation of the original languages of Hebrew and Greek in which the Bible had been written, all helped to bring about the Reformation, as did the political changes which were taking place at that time in the emerging nation states of Europe. But when all these things are taken into consideration the dominant factor was still religious experience fused with the truth of Biblical doctrine, first of all in the life of Martin Luther, but almost simultaneously in the experience of many others on the continent of Europe and in England.

There was at the time, a great yearning for reformation in the Church and in the world, for legal, moral and administrative reformation. Erasmus, the great humanist, was representative of that movement, but the change came eventually not through those channels, but through biblical doctrine, through the rediscovery of the true Gospel in Scripture. This should impress upon us, in these days when doctrine is little regarded, its importance and significance as the primary religious force in the church: nothing can be achieved where doctrine is neglected. It is no coincidence that Luther was a Doctor of Holy Scripture, appointed to teach the Bible to the students at Wittemberg. It was in the course of his lectures on the Psalms and, particularly, the Epistle to the Romans, that Luther rediscovered the real message of the Gospel that was to set him free.

The question that had dogged Luther, and had given him no peace from the time that he entered a monastery, was that which is central to all religious experience, and rightly understood is the basic question man has to resolve, 'how can I be right with God?' The answer the church gave, which his superiors and mentors gave, was not an answer that satisfied Luther. When they had exhorted him to use the sacraments, to confess his sins and receive absolution, there was nothing more they could suggest, except that he was overscrupulous and ought not to be so hard upon himself. Luther found the answer to his quest, not in the teaching of the church, but in the Bible, in the Epistle to the Romans which he was expounding to his students. There he discovered that the righteousness of God, of which Paul speaks in Romans 3, is not that passive attribute of God's character which condemns us, but the active righteousness of God in Christ by which we are saved.

Luther had been conditioned by the teaching of the church to consider the righteousness by which we are saved as something in man, something created in us by the grace of the sacraments, a righteousness of good works which sacramental grace enables us to perform, and by which God accepts us. Such righteousness continually eluded him. He felt he could never be good enough to attain such a standard. But then he saw by reading the Epistle to the Romans that this was not the sort of righteousness which was required. The righteousness of God which is revealed in the Gospel is not our own at all. It is the righteousness of God—the perfect righteousness of the Lord Jesus Christ—and it is given to all who believe as a free gift. This righteousness is never our own, but it is freely 'imputed', or counted, to those who trust in Christ as Saviour. This meant that the Gospel was, indeed, what it said it was, 'Good News'. If man had to establish his own righteousness, even with the help of God, it was not good news, because he could not do it on those terms. But this meant that God was more than a helper of sinners, He was a Saviour.

Luther described his experience in the following words, 'When I understood that the righteousness of God is not that by which he punishes us but that by which he saves us, my soul felt like a bird that was released from its cage and immediately flew up into the the the heavens'. The Gospel spelt freedom, for that which man now did in obedience to the law of God he did freely; not as something that was required to justify him before God, but as a service of love and filial obedience. One of Luther's earliest tracts, *The Liberty of the Christian Man*, sets out this freedom which the believer experiences.

Conflict with the Church

Luther did not imagine that the answer he had discovered would bring him into conflict with the Pope and the church. When in 1517 he was confronted with the sale of indulgences in his own parish and saw the spiritual harm it did in leading people to believe that they could purchase salvation with money, by buying the merits of the saints to atone for their sins or the sins of those in purgatory, he fully believed that this practice represented only an abuse of the doctrine of indulgences. He believed, when he published his 95 theses against the abuses, that he would have an ally in the Pope. He even prepared an appeal to the Pope when Cardinal Cajetan called on him to recant his views. Gradually, Luther discovered that the doctrine of justification by faith, which he had found in the Bible, brought him into conflict not merely with the abuses of the church, but with the fundamental principle of papal and priestly authority and power.

In being asked to recant and submit to the authority of the Pope Luther was faced with a painful choice. It was, however, one which he was compelled to resolve in favour of the authority of Scripture. He could not deny his experience of salvation, which he had derived from his reading of Holy Scripture. That to him was axiomatic and basic. If he were to deny that it would be tantamount to denying his

21

own existence. The matter came to a head in the disputation with John Eck at Leipzig in 1518. Luther began by denying that the primacy of the Pope was founded by divine decree in Scripture. He ended by affirming that even a council of the church could err, as it had done in the Council of Constance by condemning John Huss and his evangelical doctrines. Thus Luther was emancipated from the last remaining human authority and recognised from that point no authority but that of Scripture. That authority was self-authenticating in his experience of salvation. The objective truth of God's Word had been sealed upon his mind and heart by the inward affirmation of the Holy Ghost.

Anatomy of Protestantism

These facts we have briefly referred to give us the anatomy of Protestantism and its reason for existing over against Rome. In all the classical Protestant doctrine of the period you will find fused together both Scripture and experience. Melanchthon, Luther's colleague, criticised medieval theology for being speculative. The scholastic theologians, he said, had been discussing the question of the unity of God, the Trinity, the mystery of creation and the mode of the Incarnation for centuries but without any practical benefit. 'Have they not', he asks, 'as St Paul says, "become vain in their imaginations" while they have been trifling all their lives about universals, formalities, connotations and I know not what other inane words and expressions? But', he says, 'as to the other *loci* [passages] respecting the power of sin, the law and grace, I do not know how a man can expect to be called a Christian who is ignorant of them. For it is from these that Christ is properly known, if at least the true knowledge of Christ is to know His benefits, and not as the schoolmen teach to know His natures and the modes of His Incarnation. Unless you know for what purpose He assumed our flesh and was nailed to the cross, what benefit will it be to know His history? St Paul in his Epistle to the Romans, when he wrote a compendium of Christian doctrine, did not philosophise about the mysteries of the Trinity, about the mode of Incarnation, about active and passive creation. What is it that he treats of? Certainly of the law, of sin, of grace, which are the topics on which alone the knowledge of Christ depends'.

The Reformers had grasped the essence of the Gospel preached by Paul in the Epistle to the Romans. They recognised that it was the only answer to man's need of salvation. It was burned into their experience in letters of fire. By contrast they were terrified by the remoteness of medieval theology from the depth of human need.

The Nature of Sin

The Augsburg Confession, which was the first attempt to express systematically the biblical doctrines the Reformers had discovered, begins characteristically with a statement of original sin. They did not approach the subject as a technical theological doctrine, but from the practical need to express the inability of man to do anything that is pleasing to God, or that merits salvation. This was something which they found stated in Scripture, but also it was something which they had experienced, something which Luther had encountered again and again in his search for justification. They argued that the fall of man had not merely impaired human nature spiritually and morally, but ruined it. Man was, 'very far gone from original righteousness', and incapable of turning to God. It was not just a part of human nature that was disordered by sin—the lower nature or natural appetites, but the whole of man, his reason, his will and his affections. The effects of the Fall upon man's nature were total.

Here again the Reformers considered that the teaching of the church was not merely speculative but lacked seriousness. It did not weigh with sufficient gravity the effects of sin upon man's nature. There was a certain levity in the way in which it was argued that man could do works that merited grace. The church tended to treat the symptoms not the disease. It spoke chiefly of sins, but said little of the principle or root of sin and evil in the heart of man which tainted every work he did. In grasping the message of Romans, the Reformers had recovered the biblical doctrine of sin. The church of the Middle Ages, in following Aristotle, had taught that good works make a good and righteous man. But this was to put the cart before the horse.

The Reformers recognised in the Bible a different principle, which is, 'Either make the tree good, and his fruit good; or else make the tree corrupt, and his fruit corrupt: for the tree is known by his fruit . . . A good man out of the good treasure of the heart bringeth forth good things: and an evil man out of the evil treasure bringeth forth evil things' (Matthew 12:33, 35). As long as the principle of sin remains untouched and unchanged in the heart and mind, outward works of penance, fasting and charity do no good. The Bible speaks of *phronēma sarkos*, 'the mind of the flesh', or 'the carnal mind' which is emnity against God', this is the root cause of sin which must be dealt with before there can be any significant change in the individual, and before he can do anything that is good in the sight of God. What is needed therefore is not any mere outward change, but inward moral and spiritual regeneration. A patching up of the exterior will not do; man must become a new creature.

But how could this be brought about? Not, as the church claimed, through the sacramental system, which was sunk in mechanical and superstitious notions of grace. It could only be accomplished by the Word of God. That was the experience of the Reformers. It was the Word which had quickened faith in them. 'God, who commanded the light to shine out of darkness, hath shined in our hearts, to give the light of the knowledge of the glory of God in the face of Jesus Christ' (2 Corinthians 4:6). The creative word of Genesis is also the regenerative Word of the Gospel which constitutes man a new creature, and creates faith in him where formerly there was spiritual darkness. This was the experience of the Reformers arising directly out of their encounter with the Word. It was also the corroborative testimony of Scripture to the power of the Word in the Gospel, 'Faith cometh by hearing, and hearing by the Word of God' (Romans 10:17). The Word has the power to quicken the heart and create faith, and it is this new principle of faith which counteracts sin. In biblical terms the opposite of sin is not virtue but faith, 'for whatsoever is not of faith is sin' (Romans 14:23).

Thus the thought of the Reformers offered an anatomy of man's nature in spiritual terms which was seen to be true both biblically and experientially. This had a powerful and convincing effect. It made doctrine come alive. It gave it a human face. It was no longer a mere speculative pass-time, nor some tale of what took place in far-off times. It was saving truth embodied and alive. It was indeed God's coming down in human form to deliver man in his need.

What had emerged from the white heat of the Reformation experience was capable later, in a more reflective state, of being fashioned into a system. The basic principles were taken and set out in logical order, though not necessarily in the order in which they had arisen in experience. All the great confessions of Protestantism display a remarkable similarity and agreement in the main points of doctrine. We find running through them all, whether it be the 39 Articles, the Augsburg Confession, or the Westminster Confession, four basic principles: Scripture alone, grace alone, faith alone, the glory of god alone.

Scripture alone

This was not a dry academic principle which the Reformers sought to vindicate over against Rome. It was the message of the Bible which had been rediscovered as the saving Word and the only answer to man's need. If Scripture were threatened from any other source, be it papal authority which required Luther to retract his writings on justification by faith, or extra-biblical tradition which sought to modify or change that doctrine, then the sole sufficiency and authority of Scripture had to be maintained in the face of all opposition. To concede anything else would be to jeopardize the Gospel.

The article on Scripture holds therefore a prominent place as the basis on which any true system of doctrine must rest. The Augsburg Confession, the earliest of the

Protestant Confessions, had begun with the doctrine of original sin, because that was the order of the Reformers' experience, but the logical order necessary for a system must begin with the doctrine of Scripture, and this is reflected in the 39 Articles of the Church of England. Scripture is the source and authority from which the experience of salvation derives.

Luther was jealous for the unique authority of Scripture and defended it not only against the Pope, but also against the spirituals and anabaptists who insisted that the inner illumination and revelation of the Holy Spirit superseded that of Scripture. An attack from either side threatened the true Gospel, the sole basis of which lay ultimately in the authority of the Bible.

The 39 Articles begin the Doctrines of Salvation typically with a formal statement to the effect that Scripture is the sole and sufficient authority in all matters of faith. What therefore cannot be proved from Scripture is not necessary for faith and salvation.

The true position of any Protestant church (and that includes the Church of England, for no one until recent times and the rise of the Tractarian movement, questioned the status of the Church of England as a Protestant Reformed church), is that it takes its stand on Scripture alone. The fact that we accept and use the three great creeds does not in any way affect this, because as the Articles say, they are to be accepted because they can be proved by most certain warrant of Holy Scripture. In other words everything must rest upon Scripture, and if anything cannot be proved to be so grounded it is not to be required to be believed.

Sometimes it is said that the position of the Church of England is that it accepts a mutiple authority of Scripture, tradition, and reason. In the case of tradition this, as we have shown, is not so. The creeds are tradition, and everything else in tradition, such as the teaching of the Fathers of the first four centuries, is only accepted if it is shown to be in agreement with Scripture. Thus tradition does not constitute an independent authority.

The same is true of reason. Any principles or teaching based upon reason have no authority unless they conform to the Word of God. That is not to say that the Reformers despised reason. They probably held it in higher regard than does the present age. They recognised that a rational mind was necessary to work out the implications of revelation in the Bible. Reformed theology is just such a system of deductions and inferences from revealed truth. But no speculation of the human mind can be invested with the same authority as the Word of God, and where the two conflict at any point, human reason must give way and the Bible maintained as the only authority in matters of faith. Thus the classical position of Protestantism, in which the Church of England shares, is that the Bible is the sole authority.

Faith alone

We have seen how the Reformers were overwhelmed with a sense of sin with which the sacramental and penitential system of the church at that time was unable to cope. It was precisely this breakdown of the system which had led Luther to look outside it, and to find the message of salvation in Scripture. The more they examined their consciences the less they found that could in any sense, be regarded as good and acceptable to God. The idea that man could do works that merited grace, and that similar works added further grace, until some kind of righteousness was fashioned by human effort became wholly repugnant to them.

Yet the conviction of sin which made them despair of themselves contained the seed of their deliverance, for what was this awareness of the utter sinfulness of the human heart but the regenerating work of the Holy Spirit? This was God at work in them, and the step of faith in Christ which followed sprang from the realization of this truth about their own nature. It made them open to the truth of the Gospel, that Christ's righteousness alone is the justification of the sinner, not anything in himself. Yet he is not ready or able to take this step of faith until he has absolutely despaired of anything that he can do. Until then he clings to any rag of self-righteousness in the hope that it might be sufficient to cover his nakedness. Repentance is the recognition of what we really are, and faith the gift of trusting, not in ourselves, but in the promise of the Gospel, which is that God justifies the ungodly through faith in Christ.

It is not difficult to see how this conception of things broke the mould of the sacramental system which prevailed in the church. Regeneration is not effected *ex opere operato* by the sacrament of baptism, but, as the Reformers maintained, regeneration is repentance and is effected by the Word of God working upon the mind and conscience with the convicting and convincing power of the Holy Spirit. Thus the Word replaces the sacraments as the instrument of regeneration. But it also took priority over the sacraments in every other respect. It was trust in the promise of the Gospel that brought deliverance and justification to the sinner, not the repeated infusion of grace by the sacraments.

Yet the sacraments did not thereby become redundant as far as the Reformers were concerned. Baptism and the Lord's Supper had been instituted by divine command. They were however subordinate to, and dependent upon, the word. Luther said they were, 'a visible Word', and Calvin spoke of them as adjuncts of the Word. Their meaning was that apart from the promise of the Gospel they were meaningless, and degenerated into dumb ceremonies which ministered not to faith but to superstition. Faith held fast the promise of the Gospel, and in the light of that promise received the sacraments as divine pledges and assurances of the benefits of Christ's atoning death. But apart from the Word and apart from faith they could minister no grace.

Thus, contrary to the practice of the church in the Middle Ages, preaching was regarded as the principal office of salvation. Without it there could ordinarily be no faith. Nothing could be put in the place of preaching and its decay could only herald the decline of the church. 'This office of preaching', said Latimer, 'is the only ordinary way that God hath appointed to save us all by. Let us maintain

28

this, for I know none other; neither think I God will appoint or devise any other'.

Grace alone

Here we must be careful not to suggest that the church at that period did not believe in grace, or even teach that salvation was all of grace. It was the meaning that was attached to the word grace, and how grace was conceived of as working in the sacramental system of the church and in the individual that was the important thing. All this led to such a distortion of the real significance of grace in biblical terms as to vitiate its true meaning. Because of the church's insistence that the sacraments worked of themselves automatically (*ex opere operato*) without faith, grace came to be conceived of as some kind of impersonal power that was communicated to the recipient, and capable of enabling him to perform good works which would lead to his justification. Man's salvation was therefore of grace, it was argued, because it was with the help of grace that man was enabled to become just. However, in the course of this reasoning grace had undergone a radical change such as to destroy its real character, as had also the term justification. Neither bore any resemblance to their biblical significance, and Luther refused to recognise this as grace at all. It was a travesty, he said, for which the Almighty should not be held responsible.

Grace, as the Reformers discovered from their study of the Scriptures, is the free mercy of God, it is a gift bestowed unmerited and unearned. It is divine favour prompted, not by anything in man, but solely by the divine nature. Paul's definition is the one that must guide us: 'If by grace, then is it no more of works: otherwise grace is no more grace. But if it be of works, then is it no more grace: otherwise work is no more work' (Romans 11:6). Grace cannot be earned without destroying the nature of grace. It is by definition free and unmerited. It should be quite unnecessary to talk of free grace, as it is to talk of true truth. It is a tautology. Yet a tautology can sometimes be meaningful, and it has been found necessary to talk of free grace because of man's tendency not to accept what the Bible says, viz that God's grace is free and unmerited.

That means that God bestows the gift of righteousness or justification freely upon man: not for anything that God discerns in him, not even faith, for if we make that a meritorious work which prompts the divine favour then we destroy the nature of grace. It is no longer grace, but merit. Justification is, therefore, absolutely, unconditionally free. The perfect righteousness of God accounted to man as a free gift in Jesus Christ is, Paul declared, the true Gospel revealed by God (Romans 3). Any suggestion, therefore, that man co-operates with the grace of God in some way to produce in himself a righteousness which is accepted by God is false. Though it may seem to have a semblance of fitness in terms of human notions of fair-play and just deserts, it is not what God has revealed in his Word, it is not the Gospel.

Faith is the necessary and only complement of grace, because it takes God at his word, and trusts the promise he has made, however strange it may appear to be in terms of human understanding. That is why Paul takes Abraham as the example of faith in Romans 4 because he believed the promise of God '. . . and being not weak in faith . . . he staggered not at the promise of God through unbelief; but was strong in faith, giving glory to God' (Romans 4:19–21).

A most important feature of the doctrine of justification by faith is that it attributes the whole of man's salvation to God. It is not grounded on anything in man, or that man has done. It is, as Article XI of the Church of England puts it, solely for, 'the merits of Christ', for the sake of his righteousness, that man is accepted by God, and faith is simply a recumbency, a resting upon this righteousness of God which saves. Faith does not itself contribute anything to man's salvation. It merely accepts what God freely gives. Thus faith gives glory to God.

The Glory of God alone

Since man's salvation is wholly attributable to God, this puts God at the centre. The doctrine of justification by faith, like the doctrine of the Bible as a whole, is God-centred. Since the ground of salvation is not to be found in man, but solely in God, that which distinguishes the believer from the unbeliever is likewise to be attributed to the will and purpose of God. It was inevitable therefore that since all the Reformers shared in common the doctrine of justification by faith they should also hold in common the doctrine of election. This was true of our English Reformers as it was of Luther, Calvin and Zwingli on the continent. They were all impelled by Scripture and experience to come to this conclusion.

If one man believes the Gospel and another does not, but rejects it, to what are we to attribute this distinction? Is it because there is something good in the believer and not in the unbeliever? Is it due to the believer's effort, his striving, his resolve? If it were so, the free grace of God, which is the corner stone of justification by faith, would be vitiated. We would be back with the man-centred theology of good works, merit and deserving. The ground of the distinction, therefore, between the believer and the unbeliever must not be anything in himself, but in God. It must be God's choice, God's will, God's election that causes one man to differ from another. If experience compelled the Reformers to think thus, they had not far to go to find that this was exactly how Paul wrote about the subject. That we are chosen by God, he argues in Ephesians 1, is not attributable to anything in ourselves: the reason for it must be found in the will and purpose of God. This is something which God has, 'purposed in himself', and since God's will is something which is ultimate, and secret to himself, we must leave the matter there. We can go no further in our reasoning and we must give the glory to God.

Thus the doctrine of election is a necessary safeguard to the doctrine of justification by faith. Without it the latter soon degenerates and slips back into a doctrine of works. Faith itself becomes a good work which enables God to accept the believer. This is unavoidable once the ground of distinction is removed from God and located in man. In biblical and experiential terms there is no middle path. The church of the Middle Ages appeared to pursue a middle path with its 'synergism', the notion of God and man working together in man's salvation, but it failed lamentably, and it was such failure that made the Reformation necessary. A man-centred theology, whether it be in popular Protestantism or Roman Catholicism, is always characterised by this division of labour between God and man. It serves only to vitiate the Gospel and to deny God the glory that belongs rightly and only to him.

Election also played another important role in the thinking of the Reformers, for it meant that the extent of the church, the true church, was determined by, and known only to, God. It could not be determined by man or any order of men. The Pope claimed enormous powers, which the church declared had been bestowed upon him as the successor of Peter by Christ, powers to bind and to loose on earth, in heaven and in hell. The triple tiara signified his authority over all three realms. The power of the papacy and the priesthood had been more closely defined in this respect by Innocent III in his decree on auricular confession, and by Boniface VIII in his bull, *Unam Sanctam*. To belong to the true church, according to the traditional teaching of the church, was to be in communion with the Pope; 'outside the church there is no salvation'. In the light of the doctrine of election such traditional teaching was seen to have no force. The biblical teaching pointed to the sovereignty of God in man's salvation. This had a liberating effect, for it freed men from the spiritual power and authority which had been usurped by the Pope and clergy. The doctrine of election is fatal to all ecclesiastical pretensions.

The positive message of Protestantism

It will then be clearly seen that the Reformation was, in essence, a religious movement in which the great doctrines of the Gospel, the doctrines of grace, were rediscovered and reinstated in the church. It was a positive affirmation of the cardinal truths of Scripture. It is difficult to understand how it has become branded as a negative movement. It lacks the marks of such negativity. It is, as we have seen, an integrated and coherent system of doctrine. It stands in its own right. Neither of these things is the mark of mere negation. The very word 'Protestant' at its inception supports this view. Its Latin derivation is inconsistent with a negative interpretation. It means, 'to declare publicly, to bear witness, to testify, and so to protest'. Dr Johnson considered that the predominant meaning of the word, as used in English, is of the same character. 'To protest', he says, 'is to give solemn declaration of opinion, or resolution'.

The religious use of the word 'Protestant' first occurred at the second Diet of Speiers, when the princes who supported reform affirmed their right, which they had established at the first Diet of Speiers, to order their own states along Reformed lines. They held that no majority or power could dictate to them on matters of conscience. In this they were simply doing collectively what Luther had affirmed as an individual at Worms, viz, that his conscience was bound by the Word of God, and it was to that that he had to render absolute obedience. He could do no other.

Such a positive affirmation of what God had revealed in His Word was necessary for those times, as it is for ours, and the negative attitude seems to be on the part of those who oppose such an affirmation, rather then those who testify to it. One of the first acts of the Reformers was to draw up systematic statements of the fruits of their study of Scripture in the form of Confessions. All the main churches of the Reformation are characterised by such Confessions, which are in effect the crystallisation of biblical teaching on salvation. The negative reaction was to be seen later in the Council of Trent, which sought to controvert the principal tenets of Protestant doctrine, and which gave birth to the modern Roman Catholic Church. It is possible to say that the Church of Rome, as we know it today, did not exist before the Council of Trent, but was brought into existence at that point as a result of a negative response to the positive assertion of the Gospel by the Reformers. The doctrine to which the Church of Rome pledged itself as Trent represented the triumph of an arrogant and negative faction.

It is time that the term Protestant be properly rehabilitated as representing the mainstream of biblical truth, which is essential to the maintenance of the true Gospel in the church in every age. If Protestantism dies the church dies. The candle is extinguished and the candlestick removed. The challenging days in which we are living should help us to appreciate the peril in which the church stands. The term Protestant has been despised, the doctrines of the Reformation and the classical Protestant Confessions have been neglected and ignored. This can only mean that the church is in serious and imminent danger.

3: The reconstruction of authority in Protestantism

The more I think about the conflict between Luther and the papacy, and what enabled him, in an almost unprecedented way, to oppose the might and authority of the medieval church, the more I am convinced that the source of his own strength was the *felt authority* of the Word of God. I take that expression 'felt authority' from Thomas Chalmers' Bridgwater Treatise, where he speaks of the universal experience of conscience and the moral law as a 'felt authority', ie, it is not something academic, remote from life, and purely objective. The reality and authority of conscience are something which is experienced, something which is felt by the individual when he does right or wrong, as Paul wrote of the heathen 'their conscience also bearing witness, and their thoughts the meanwhile accusing or else excusing one another' (Romans 2:15). It is not merely a matter of knowing with the mind the difference between right and wrong, but feeling in the heart the truth of these things in the activity of everyday life. That is the nature of the authority of conscience. It is a 'felt authority'.

And we may say the same of Luther, and for that matter the other Reformers too. Their experience of the authority of the Word of God was a *felt authority*. They had experienced the truth of which the Bible speaks. This word of the Gospel (and of the Law) had been brought home to their hearts and minds in the most powerful way by experience of all that it means. They had *felt* the condemnation of the Law of God, and the utter inability of the sinner to save himself. They had *felt* the truth of the Gospel, that Christ Jesus died for sinners. They *knew* by faith that they were justified by his perfect righteousness. This was something as real to them as their own personal existence. They could not doubt its truth any more than they could doubt that they were alive. And it was that, the *felt authority* of the Word, that enabled Luther to oppose the authority, the doctrines, the might of the papacy. He could not have done it on any other ground at all.

For example, what if Luther had known the Bible only as many people in the church then and today know it, namely, as a holy book; as a history of the people of God; as an account of the life, death and resurrection of Jesus Christ; but without any experience of the Gospel of justification by faith? On that basis he could not have opposed the authority of Rome. However much he might have said he believed in the authority of the Bible. However many theories he may have been acquainted with relating to its authenticity and inerrancy, without the inward conviction of its truth he would not have been able to take the stand he did. But the Word of God had been so indelibly written into his experience that he could not deny it. His words convey that, 'Here I stand. I can do no other'. He knew that this Word had saved him just as certainly as he knew that he existed. Therefore he could do no other. You cannot, and do not, talk like that about theories, propositions, arguments. If you are dealing in these you may be wrong, there is always the possibility of doubt and uncertainty, of some new fact emerging, and so on. So you may be wrong. But the felt authority and truth of the Gospel, like the truth of existence, admits of no doubt. This authority is sealed upon the heart. 'I can do no other.'

Now this is the truth by which Protestantism lives. It is not merely objective authority, based upon arguments and theories about the authority of Scripture. This is not, of course, to suggest that such arguments do not have an important place in Christian apologetic. They most certainly do. But without the experience of salvation of which the Bible speaks they are no good. They do not and cannot give Protestantism the authority that it needs today, any more than they could have given birth to the Reformation. Nor is it an authority which is purely subjective, arising from man's own experience, because that is ultimately delusory. It is the fusion of the two things—the objective truth of God's Word becoming real in the experience of the individual so that his own existence is determined by it. 'My conscience is taken captive by the Word of God. I can do no other.' Or as Paul put it, 'The life which I now live . . . I live by faith of the Son of God, who loved me, and gave himself for me' (Galatians 2:20). My life is now so conditioned and penetrated by the truth of God's Word in the Gospel of Christ, that I cannot deny it any more than I can deny myself—that I am. That is the unique authority of Protestantism, because it is the unique authority of authentic Christianity, and anything else, every substitute, is spurious, and a delusion, which is ultimately demonic, because it pretends to an authority which belongs only to God and his Word.

Erroneous paths to authority

Papal power and authority are demonic because they represent the absolute objectification of power, and call for the complete surrender of the mind and will of the individual to it. They call on the individual to abdicate his responsibilities as an individual and accept the mind and will of another in his place. Implicit faith is the doctrine that is bound up with this understanding of authority. The individual must assent to everything that the church and the Pope, as infallible teach, even though he may not know what that teaching is. This is why this authority is demonic and ultimately destructive. It is akin to the authority of dictatorship in the political sphere, where individuals and a nation submit themselves to the will and judgment of a dictator, a leader who claims to embody the will and mind of the people. That is why Roman Catholic countries have been breeding grounds for political dictatorship. The authority of the Pope if conceded represents the rape of the individual conscience, and the substitution for it of a power that is external to it. The surrender of the conscience in this way can only be attended by perilous consequences. To say, 'I am commanded to do it, and have no alternative but to obey' has, as we have seen in the history of the last war, produced terrible and disastrous results. Yet that is the kind of authority the papacy in its essence represents. It is of that genre or type of external, objective authority which overrides and overrules the individual conscience and is hence demonic.

The second type of authority is that where the individual seeks the seat of authority in himself alone. The humanism that accompanied the Reformation led to this search for a ground of certainty and authority in man that was independent of revelation. Thus Descartes sought an indubitable ground of certainty within experience and claimed that he had found it in the fact of doubt itself. Man can doubt everything but he cannot doubt that fact that he is doubting. 'I think therefore I am.' He had found, he believed, the ground of absolute certainty and authority within himself. This conviction has been reiterated in many different ways in the centuries since, in the empiricism, rationalism and existentialism of the modern age. They are basically variations on the same humanistic theme. The burden of it is always the same: that man is the centre and measure of things and that ultimate truth is to be found within man's experience; that revelation, the Bible, may serve to confirm or illustrate the truth which man has discovered in his mind or his experience, but does not add anything to it, or communicate anything new. Thus man asserts his autonomy, his independence of God and the Word of God and affirms that his authority is within himself.

But this too is demonic, for it again usurps the authority and prerogative of the Word of God, and ascribes it to the individual's experience. As the political counterpart of papalism is dictatorship so the counterpart of individualism is anarchy. It acts as a corrosive in society leading to its disintegration. It sets man against man. We are witnessing the effects of modern humanism in the moral decline of our society today; in the 'situation ethic' which declares that if you feel a thing is right it is right. The ultimate arbiter is the subjective experience of the individual. The attempt to rescue man from this complete atomisation or fragmentation of society is seen in the endeavour to arrive at a consensus of minds or experience, to arrive at the lowest common denominator. But the principle underlying this is really the same, namely, that the authority which is appealed to is still something within man. It is still a subjective standard of authority.

The true understanding of authority derived from the Reformation, which is the fusion of experience with the objective standard and truth of God's Word, is *not* reflected in our society today. And so in its absence we are faced with dictatorship or chaos, spiritual and political authoritarianism or anarchy, the one, the spiritual, being the progenitor of the other, the political.

Recovery of authority through doctrinal renewal

The path therefore to the reinstatement of the Reformation concept of authority must be the recovery of the religious faith and experience of the Reformers. Without that we shall not have a firm base, and anything we seek to do will simply be like preserving the shell without the kernel, which it is the purpose of the shell to protect. We must recapture the living religion of the Reformers if we are to recover the true authority and freedom that belong to Protestantism. And the path to the recovery of that living religion is the path of doctrinal renewal. The task to which we must give ourselves is the recovery of the distinctive doctrines of Protestantism, for the life and experience and authority of Protestantism cannot be maintained without them, whether it be in the church or in society. (It goes without saying that the regeneration of society must begin with the regeneration of the church.)

Now talk about doctrine may seem to many people to be a dry and arid thing, and about as far removed from life as one could imagine. This is the reason why many groups concerned with renewal eschew doctrine as lifeless and obstructive of life. They are of course wrong, for religion cannot long maintain itself without theology any more than the human body could maintain itself without the bone structure. Religion without theology quickly degenerates into mere sentiment and emotion. The Reformers did not look upon doctrine as dry and lifeless but, on the contrary, saw it as the real source of power in religion, and of religious faith.

At a time when many were seeking moral reformation of the abuses of the church and society, Luther sought a doctrinal reformation because he saw that it was that which was fundamentally wrong. 'As early as 1515', says Ranke, 'it is clear that he considered that the root of corruption in the church and the world was to be ascribed to the priests who declared to the people too many maxims and fables of human invention, and not the pure Word of God. "For", he said, "the Word of life alone is able to work out the regeneration of man". . . Even then Luther looked for the salvation of the world far less to an amendment of life, which was only secondary in his eyes, than to the revival of true doctrines, and there was none with which he was so penetrated as that of justification by faith.' In this he differed from Erasmus who sought only to reform the abuses of the church. Luther said, 'Others have attacked the Pope's morals, I have attacked his doctrine'. It was doctrine which reformed the church and changed the face of Europe in the sixteenth century. Why should we imagine that it will be any different today?

If things are wrong in the church and society today we may safely conclude it is because things have gone wrong doctrinally, because the true doctrines of the Bible are not being taught and even possibly are not known by those who should teach them. Justification by faith, said Luther, is the doctrine by which the church is seen to be standing or falling, ie, if it is understood, believed, experienced and preached, the church is spiritually alive and effective, but if it is neglected, despised, set aside, or even unknown then the church falls. The church then becomes subject to demonic forces and demonic structures of authority whether it be of the authoritarian or anarchic kinds. And the same is true of society, for, where the church is weak and corrupt, society is left a prey to the same destructive and enslaving powers.

So it is quite wrong to imagine that doctrine has nothing to do with life, and the task to which we must give ourselves if we wish to see true authority restored in Protestantism is the task of the revival of the doctrines of Protestantism. And how else can this be done except by preaching? Publishing and writing can undoubtedly play a part as they always have, and a very important part as we know from the history of publishing at the time of the Reformation and since. But I do not think this is the primary means. Preaching must be, and must remain, the principal means of doctrinal renewal. The small importance attached to preaching today in the church is itself another symptom of the doctrinal decline of which we are speaking. It is a sign that something has gone radically wrong in the church, for if we understood and valued the place of doctrine, preaching would hold the highest place in our personal priorities and those of the church generally. Other ages than ours have understood this. Queen Elizabeth I evidently appreciated this point for she is said to have 'tuned' her pulpits, ie, she ensured that only certain things were taught from them and not others. The pulpits of the Church of England today are badly in need of tuning. Alas, perhaps it is true to say that the office or organ of preaching is so badly decayed that it is in need of something more than tuning— it needs rebuilding. We must communicate to the church again the importance of preaching, but that will only be possible when we appreciate once more the importance of doctrine and its vital role in the life and well-being of the church and, indeed, of society as a whole.

But think what a unique opportunity is afforded the church by its thousands of pulpits up and down the country. There is no other institution or organisation equipped with such means of teaching and communicating week by week certain principles and doctrines to the people. We have the machinery for reformation available. If it could be harnessed to the purpose of communicating the truth of God, so that the distinctive doctrines of the Reformation

41

become once again the experience of both preachers and hearers, then we would be well on the way to the recovery of the distinctive authority of Protestantism, which resides in the fusion of individual experience with the truth of God's Word. When this becomes real in the experience of the individual, so real that he can no more doubt it than he can his own existence, then you have the basis for that authority which determines the life of both the individual and the society that accepts it.

Preaching the great doctrines of Protestantism does not mean giving them to people undiluted. You can preach them over and over again by preaching from the Bible passages in the lectionary or the Epistle and Gospel as Latimer did. You do not have to take learned tomes into the pulpit. People do not have to be choked with theology. As Spurgeon said of the 'five points' of Calvinism: they are like lumps of sugar, to be taken in tea, not eaten whole. And so we must always be reiterating the themes of justification by faith, and so forth, but in such a way as not to weary people but refresh them because we ourselves are refreshed by them.

Now if this were done again, as it was at the time of the Reformation; if the church were fired with the vision of so communicating God's Word as to make it, through the power of the Holy Ghost, the living experience and religious faith of the people, then it would begin to renew the heart of the nation, the blood would begin to circulate once more in the veins, and health and colour return to the cheeks. The powers of anarchy and dictatorship from the left and the right, which threaten a sick society, would begin to retreat before the resurgence of life and power at the centre. The Word of God is after all the Word of Life, and when its truth is imbibed and absorbed into the bloodstream of the nation, when its truth is fused with the experience of a people, then it must restore the corporate life of the nation.

In the church many clergy are no longer sure of the way to go. Anglo-Catholicism, despite appearances, is largely a spent force. The rank and file of the clergy are unsure of

Roman Catholicism as a commitment. All the expedients seem to have failed. There is a doctrinal vacuum in the church. If there were sufficient people with sufficient un-aninmity, conviction, and seriousness to address themselves to this situation and say clearly and distinctly that the Protestant way is the right way and the only way; that the distinctive doctrines of the Reformation are the teaching of the Word of God and are our only salvation, it could meet with a positive response. As Protestants we must recover our nerve, our confidence in our message. We must be sure of our authority as Luther was of his, 'I can do no other'. And when we are so assured we must expect the Word to bring forth a reformation in the church and in the world as it did in Luther's day.

The Pattern of Reformation

Today one detects a certain pessimism amongst people. How can the authority which has been broken down and destroyed—the authority of the parent, the teacher, the magistrate—ever be restored? There is a feeling of inevit-ability about the growing anarchy and fragmentation of our society that is taking place, as if the forces of history were compelling us to move further and further in that direction, and there were nothing we can do about it. But we fail to see that the 'inevitability' lies not in any historical process, but in the choice that we have freely made as a society to adopt a humanist, secular philosophy of life in which the only authority which is recognised is that which resides in man, in the individual. Once you have taken that step, of course, the working out of the consequences in society are inevitable, but we should recognise this, and see that we are victims of our own deliberate folly, not of the so-called historical process, or fate, or some such notion of the world and history.

Of course, there are those who, like the Marxists, and others, have a vested interest in telling us that all this is inevitable, that it is the onward march of history and we must accept it; and there are those who are foolish enough to believe them. But this is not so, and we can see it is not so if we take the trouble to think about it. The nemesis that is overtaking us is the direct consequence of the godless, humanistic philosophy that has been adopted by the Western world.

There is no inevitable reason, however, why our civilization should sink in chaos and anarchy, or succumb to the appeal of the dictator or, in the spiritual realm, the blandishments of the Pope. There is a third possibility that is open to us if we will accept it, and that is the authority of Protestantism, which resides in the living experience of the Word of God, in the self-authenticating truth of the Bible. Where the saving power of God's Word is experienced, as it was at the Reformation, it recreates man as a responsible being under authority, as answerable to divine authority. It also reconstitutes and reconstructs society. As there are demonic and destructive consequences that inevitably follow upon the rejection of God's Word, and these work themselves out in society, so there are saving influences that follow upon the acceptance of God's Word and, with a similar inevitability, work themselves out in society.

This is why we cannot accept the argument that the Bible must be adapted and conformed to the prevailing culture of the age in which we live for it to be effective. That produces the very opposite result. It emasculates the Word of God and makes it of 'none effect'. That was the charge our Lord brought against the Pharisees; they were, 'making the word of God of none effect through your tradition' (Mark 7:13). You have adapted it and accommodated it to the needs of your age and the circumstances of your time, and so rendered it weak and powerless. St Paul says the same, 'For Christ sent me . . . to preach the Gospel: not with wisdom of words, lest the cross of Christ should be made of none effect' (1 Corinthians 1:17). The wisdom, culture, ingenuity, philosophy of the world can rob the Word of its power and effect, especially when we seek to make its message conformable to worldly structures. That is why we must affirm the Word in all its primitive authority and spiritual power. And we must do this precisely because the Word is capable of changing structures, of changing society, and creating a culture which arises directly out of its own doctrines and principles. We seem to have forgotten that it is the Word that turns the world upside down, and now we seem anxious to turn the Word upside down to make it conformable to the world. The commission of God to the prophet is, 'Behold, I have put my words in thy mouth. See, I have this day set thee over the nations and over the kingdoms, to root out, and to pull down, and to destroy, and to throw down, to build, and to plant' (Jeremiah 1:9, 10).

Where the living authority and power of the Word of God is felt and experienced in a community, it throws down the destructive, demonic culture and structures and creates new ones of order and authority. It is a mistake to treat the structures and culture of any society as something given, into which the Word of God must be made to fit. The Word must be understood to be capable of regenerating and creating anew the community, the nation into which it comes in power. This surely is the presupposition from which any reconstruction of authority must begin either in society or in the church today.

Perhaps no better example of this principle at work can be given than that of the Reformation itself. The success of that movement did not depend upon adapting the Word to the culture of the age. That had been going on in the centuries that preceded the Reformation when the Scriptures had been accommodated to a culture based upon the Thomist/Aristotelean philosophy. The consequence of this was the corruption and distortion of the biblical message of salvation. What the Reformation did was to break the mould, to set the Word of God free. Thus the Word created its own forms and structures as it swept away the old culture and introduced a new. Art, science, literature, and music were all regenerated by this great movement. A new society, a new civilization emerged under the impact of the Word of God. All of which proves that the Word must have priority. 'Pray', says St Paul, 'that the word of the Lord may have free course, and be glorified' .(Where then the power and authority of the Word of God are felt it is capable

45

of recreating not only the individual but society itself. 'If any man be in Christ he is a new creation' (2 Corinthians 5:17). That regenerating power can also be felt by the community, for 'the leaves of the tree [of life] were for the healing of the nations'.

Summary of argument

Protestantism arises out of a living encounter with the Word of God. It is a positive and coherent system of teaching existing in its own right and based upon Scripture alone. It is not merely a negative protest against Rome, and if the Roman Catholic Church ceased to exist the truth of Protestantism would still live on. Where Protestantism is threatened, the true spiritual life of the church is threatened.

The authority of Protestantism is a 'felt authority', ie, it is the fusion of the objective truth of God's Word with the experience of the individual, in such a way that he can no more deny it than he can deny his own existence. It was this which made the Reformation possible, and it is this which must be the driving force in the reformation of the church and the world today. There is no short cut! We can only recover authority by recovering the living religion of the Reformation and of the Bible. The attempt to seek authority by other means is illusory and will result in the emergence of demonic structures of authority such as dictatorship and anarchy.

Papalism and the retreat into pre-Reformation forms of authority in the church appeal to many today as a quick, expedient answer to the problem, but they will be attended with disastrous consequences.

The splitting of the 'felt authority' of Protestantism into objective authority alone without experience of the truth, or, alternatively, experience without the objective truth of God's Word are not real options for Protestantism, and have destructive and enslaving tendencies for the individual and society.

The only real path is that of recapturing the living faith and power of true religion based upon the truth of God's Word. The essential step towards that rebirth of Protestantism is doctrinal renewal in the church. We must give ourselves to the task of restoring to their proper place the great doctrines of the Protestant Reformation, which are the doctrines of Scripture. That can only be done by restoring the office of preaching. We have all the machinery of reformation. It must be harnessed to the task.

Finally, we must not be intimidated by current fashionable trends into thinking that the Word of God must be made to fit into the culture and presuppositions of the present age in order to become meaningful and effective. The Word has priority over culture; it can and does create its own culture which is superior. And that is what our church and society need today.

Let us therefore have faith in God. 'O God, we have heard with our ears, and our fathers have declared unto us, the noble works that thou didst in their days, and in the old time before them. O Lord, arise, help us, and deliver us for thy Name's sake.'

4: Has Rome really changed?

It is impossible to appreciate the nature of Roman Catholicism today without some understanding of the Council of Trent, which opened in 1545 to deal with the doctrinal problems raised by Luther and the Reformation. Prior to Trent attempts had been made to resolve the differences between the two sides, the most important of which was the Conference of Ratisbon (1541). In view of the present attempts to find doctrinal agreement between Protestantism and Roman Catholicism it is worth reminding ourselves that similar efforts have been made before. In fact, the technique employed was the same as that in use today, viz the attempt to invest words with a double meaning which will conceal the doctrinal differences between the parties.

At Ratisbon the subject under discussion was that which had given rise to the Reformation, justification. Large concessions were made by the Roman Catholic side, but one term was reserved and wrapped up in ambiguous language. That term was 'faith'. 'Faith alone', they said they agreed to, but by faith they meant the ground of a personal righteousness by which the believer would be justified. So, nothing in fact was conceded by the Roman Catholic acceptance of the words 'faith alone', because by their definition of faith they reintroduced the very thing which was meant to be excluded, viz an inherent righteousness as the basis of man's acceptance with God. Luther's words to Melanchthon were, 'Popish writers pretend that they have always taught what we now teach, concerning faith and good works, and that they are unjustly accused of the contrary. Thus the wolf puts on sheep's skin until he gains admission into the fold?

Trent had the merit of washing its hands of the attempt to find such compromises by which the two sides might appear to be reconciled. The Pope and the council had come to the conclusion that the time for placating Protestants had passed. What was needed was the clear formulation of Catholic doctrine and the unqualified condemnation of the (supposed) errors of the Reformation. This policy served to bring out on the surface what was latent in the Reformation situation, which was, that the two sides represented not merely different emphases, or, as some have since maintained, just verbal misunderstandings, but two mutually exclusive systems of doctrine—the one based upon Scripture alone and the other upon Scripture and tradition.

This came to light in the council's treatment of the Rule of Faith. The attempt to answer the Reformers from Scripture alone had been found to fail. Trent adopted the only recourse if the traditional teachings of the church were to be justified, and that was to make Scripture and tradition of equal authority. The effect of this upon subsequent relations between Catholicism and Protestantism were decisive. The reconciliation of the two was henceforth impossible. A handful of bishops with sympathy towards the Lutheran position argued against it, but it made no difference. Once the decree had been made all the other decisions of the Council flowed from it. The system and theology of Roman Catholicism rests ultimately, as Protestants must view it, upon a non-biblical source which is inauthentic and fallible. The decree of Vatican I 300 years later on the infallibility of the Pope, was in a sense the inevitable outcome of what had been initiated at Trent. Tradition, if it is to be a source of the church's doctrine, must not only be appealed to alongside Scripture but must also be invested with an authority and character equal to that of Scripture. Hence the need was felt increasingly in the period between Trent and Vatican I to declare tradition at its source and head in the papacy, as infallible.

Trent also dealt with justification. Luther's doctrine of

'justification by faith only' was regarded as being at the root of most of his 'errors' on the sacraments, the power of the keys, indulgences and purgatory. The debate in the council turned upon the difference between imparted righteousness, the Catholic doctrine, and imputed righteousness, the Protestant doctrine. The latter was rejected by 32 votes to 5. Its clear and unequivocal rejection was stated in canons XI and XII of the decree:

> If anyone saith that men are justified either by the sole imputation of the righteousness of Christ, or by the sole remission of sins, to the exclusion of the grace and the charity which are poured forth into their hearts by the Holy Ghost, and is inherent in them, or even that the grace whereby we are justified is only the favour of God, let him be anathema.
> If anyone saith that justifying faith is nothing else but faith in the divine mercy which remits sins for Christ's sake, or that this faith alone is that whereby we are justified, let him be anathema.

But this is exactly what Luther believed and taught. Moreover, it was not just Luther's opinion, but what he found St Paul teaching in the epistle to the Romans, and the sound interpretation behind it is something which has been proved to be valid by biblical scholarship since that time. Justification in the Bible is a legal sentence, ie, it is the declaration by God of the sinner as righteous. It has nothing to do with his actual condition. The Church of Rome by insisting that justification means to make just, (as the Latin roots of the word might suggest), and that it therefore refers to the actual condition morally and spiritually of the person at the time of justification, was perpetuating a notion that was alien to Scripture.

The justification of which the council spoke and which the Roman Catholic Church still teaches today, is something, they say, which is communicated through baptism. By virtue of this sacrament the individual is forgiven and a new nature imparted. This grace of justification is regarded as infused or poured into the heart, as the decree states, and it is communicated *ex opere operato*, ie, the sacrament works of itself without regard to the faith of the recipient. Here of course there is a deep divide which relates not only to the point under discussion but colours the whole religious outlook that depends upon it.

The council also went on to affirm that after the consecration of the elements in the Mass our Lord Jesus Christ, very God and very man, is truly, really and substantially contained under the species of bread and wine: that in the consecration of these elements there is a conversion of the whole substance of the bread into Christ's body, and a conversion of the whole substance of the wine into the substance of his blood, so as to justify the use of the term transubstantiation, and that therefore the highest form of worship which is due to God himself is to be rendered by the faithful to the sacrament of the altar.

The sacrament of penance, the mass, purgatory and indulgences were also made the subject of decrees. But enough has been said to show how Roman Catholic doctrine was being formulated at Trent, in some cases for the first time, in reaction to the Confessions of the Reformation. The council cleared up the religious position, and left no doubt as to what henceforth was to be taught and believed by the Church of Rome. It served to fix Roman Catholic doctrine on broad and systematic lines which continue to the present time, and which were by definition exclusive of the biblical doctrines insisted on by the Reformers.

One thing not dealt with in a decree at Trent was the constitution of the church. No formal decision was pronounced with regard to the primacy of the Bishop of Rome. The council called the Roman Church the Mother and Mistress of all the churches. It also declared that the decrees of the council should have force only if the rights of Rome were upheld. Finally, in the last of its decrees the council, in fact, recognised the primacy of the Pope by submitting the decisions arrived at to papal confirmation. But the question of the nature of the primacy of the Pope, and especially whether he is subject to an ecumenical council, were not decided at Trent. They had to wait until the First Vatican Council of 1870. In that council the work of defining and formulating the teaching of Roman Catholicism, begun at

Trent, found its necessary fulfilment and completion. There papal primacy and papal infallibility together were added to form the keystone of the arch, the foundations of which had been constructed at Trent.

First Vatican Council 1870

The first Vatican Council established two things in connection with the papacy which are of profound importance to our understanding of Roman Catholicism today.

First, the primacy of the Pope, ie, that the Pope holds a primacy of absolute authority over the whole church and that this authority is direct and full. The suggestion that the authority of the Pope rests upon the authority of the church was specifically rejected. It was argued that the authority conferred by Christ on Peter and his supposed successors, the Popes, was given direct and was not given by the church.

There are those who argue that the decree of the Second Vatican Council on the church, with its emphasis upon collegiality, ie. bishops, working together with the Pope in decision making, served to qualify and moderate the isolation in which the Pope had been placed by Vatican I. But a careful study of the documents will show that this is not the case. While much is said about the bishops acting in concert to determine the mind of the church, and the Pope acting with them, yet the unique position of the Pope is safeguarded, and nothing is stated which detracts from the authority of his office as defined in Vatican I. Indeed it is plainly stated:

> All this teaching about the institution, the perpetuity, the force and reason for the sacred primacy of the Roman Pontiff and his infallible teaching authority, this sacred Synod again proposes to be firmly believed by all the faithful.

The task was one of clarification, not correction, of what had been defined at Vatican I. Indeed, by the nature of things such decrees are irreformable. A little later it is stated:

> The college or body of bishops has no authority unless it is

simultaneously conceived of in terms of its head, the Roman Pontiff, Peter's successor, and without any lessening of his power of primacy over all, pastors as well as the general faithful. For in virtue of his office, that is, as Vicar of Christ and pastor of the whole Church, the Roman Pontiff has full, supreme, and universal power over the Church. And he can always exercise his power freely.

The power ascribed to the Pope both in Vatican I and Vatican II is absolute authority over the church, over clergy and laity, in faith and morals, and there is no limit upon the freedom with which he may exercise it.

The second thing decreed by the First Vatican Council was the infallibility of the Pope. This, of course does not mean that the Pope is regarded as infallible in everything he says, but only on those rare occasions when he explicitly states that he is defining doctrine. However the ascription of infallibility is made to him for such utterances. The decree runs:

The Roman Pontiff when he speaks *ex cathedra*, that is, when exercising the office of pastor and teacher of all Christians, he defines with his supreme apostolic authority a doctrine regarding faith or morals to be held by the universal Church, through the divine assistance promised to him in St Peter, is possessed of that infallibility with which the divine Redeemer willed his Church to be endowed in defining doctrine concerning faith and morals: and therefore such definitions of the Roman Pontiff are irreformable of themselves and not from the consent of the Church.

Cardinal Guidi spoke for the liberal minority when in the debate he sought to modify the proposal by suggesting that it should be made clear in the decree that it is not the Pope alone who issues a definition, but the Pope and the bishops, whom he spoke of as 'the witnesses of tradition'. The Pope called for the Cardinal in private and upbraided him. 'Witnesses of tradition?' Pius is reported to have said, 'there's only one; that's me'.

The definitions of doctrine in Vatican I again make clear the fundamental difference between ·Roman Catholicism and Protestantism. As the Roman Catholic Bishop B. C. Butler declares in his summing up of the significance of this council: 'The defining of the position of the Pope as successor and heir of St Peter, according to the mind of the Catholic Church, and the setting forth in unmistakable terms the implications of his primacy and infallible teaching authority, was surely a right act: in that it shuts out the possibility of anyone seeking union with the Catholic Apostolic Roman Church—be it separated Eastern Orthodox Churches, or be it Christian religious bodies in the West, or individuals—doing so under misapprehension of what is involved . . . And so', Butler continues, 'the Catholic Church was honest at the First Vatican Council in laying down the lines unequivocally in regard to the papacy, as she was honest at Trent in laying down her lines in regard to the challenge of the Reformers, thus making clear to all the conditions of communion with her . . . And so the First Vatican Council takes its stand alongside of Trent as a great land mark of the life of the Church'.

We can only applaud such honesty wherever it exists, and surely it would be naive to think that anything that was decreed by these two great councils, which determined the nature, scope and direction of the teaching of the Roman Catholic Church, has been materially altered since. But that is the next question we shall try to resolve.

The Second Vatican Council

The Second Vatican Council has caused a great deal of confusion in the minds of many Protestants about whether the Church of Rome has changed or not, and what exactly she now teaches. Whenever the subject is raised in discussion, and appeal is made to the official teaching of the Church of Rome in either the Council of Trent or Vatican I it is said in response, 'Oh, but now it is different, the Church of Rome has changed', or, 'Rome doesn't teach that any more'.

A great deal of the confusion must arise from ignorance about what was really decided at Vatican II. The documents of the council are very large, and it must be presumed that very few people have actually read or studied them. Roman Catholics themselves are also confused about the real significance of the council, attributing to it things which did not originate with it. Cardinal Heenan, writing a few years after the council complained of, 'certain views which have gained currency since the Council although they do not derive from the Council. Because they have gained currency only since the Council they are thought by some . . . to be part of its teaching'. So there ought to be considerable caution on the part of Protestants in their approach to much that is claimed as change in the Church of Rome. The actual documents of Vatican II do not justify the view that many have taken, that Rome is now doctrinally a different church from what it was before the council.

There are also other factors which tend to confuse. There are for example the peripheral changes which have taken place since Vatican II. Services have been revised and are now in English, there is a new openness about the Church of Rome which is so different from the past, and there are fewer restrictions on Roman Catholics, in their relations with Christians from other churches. All these things are outward, and visible signs of change which by their nature make a considerable impact on society, but we should not therefore conclude that this means that the Roman Church has changed its fundamental doctrines.

There is also the theological ferment and debate that is going on at present in the Roman Catholic Church. Many people were made aware for the first time, by the reports of the deliberations of Vatican II, of how the decrees were formulated. They were surprised to discover that the subjects were debated and that 'progressive' bishops pressed for change and amendment in the schemata of the decrees. This was of course in itself nothing new. It had happened at Trent and at Vatican I. But it was new to very many Protestants who had never thought of the Church of Rome like this before, and it made them think that possibly great changes were in store. What they appear to have overlooked is that once the decree is formulated it then becomes the faith of the Roman Church and the opposing parties must submit. Those 'progressive' theologians who persist in their views are made to feel the displeasure of the Vatican, as has happened in the case of Hans Küng. Sometimes Protestants have mistakenly taken the views of these theologians to be the teachings of the Roman Catholic Church. This only adds to the confusion about what Vatican II has actually effected, and whether Rome has actually changed her doctrines. It is unwise to regard any academic theologian, however eminent, as speaking officially for the Church of Rome.

It would be best in approaching the work of the Council to examine again the reasons Pope John XXIII gave for calling it. Amongst those reasons is the hope that the council will provide greater doctrinal clarity regarding the position of the Church of Rome:

> . . . it is very natural that the forthcoming Council should provide premises of doctrinal clarity and of mutual charity that will make still more alive in our separated brothers the wish for the hoped-for return to unity and will smooth the way.

The purpose of the council was therefore greater clarification of the teaching of the Roman Catholic Church, not change, which was in any case ruled out by definition. It was hoped at the same time that by this work of elucidation the doctrine of the Roman Church would make its own intrinsic appeal to the separated brethren and encourage in them the desire to return to unity. Pope Paul VI took a similar view of the council and in defence of the inerrancy of the Church insisted that the reforms of the council did not involve fudamental change, least of all doctrinal change, but that the process could be compared to the pruning of a tree, cutting out dead wood but leaving the main trunk and branches intact.

But it is the basic shape and form of Roman Catholic doctrine with which we disagree, and simply exposing it more fully to view is not going to make it more attractive. The organisational and administrative reforms brought about by the council are of no consequence to us as Protestants. The downgrading of the curial departments in favour of a synod of bishops and of national conferences of hierarchies are quite separate matters from such doctrinal questions as the infallibility of the Pope, which is not touched by the Second Vatican Council. No amount of clarification or stripping away of excrescences is going to make the fundamental doctrines of Roman Catholicism more acceptable to Protestants because it is the fundamental doctrines with which we disagree. For example, the putting of the mass in English does not make it any more acceptable, because it is still the mass. The theology is unchanged.

We have here a problem which is really the same as that which existed at the time of the Reformation. At that time there were those within the Church of Rome who thought that if the abuses of the church were reformed, and the moral tone of the clergy raised, then the reason for the Reformation would disappear, and protestants would be constrained to return to the fold. But when the Counter-Reformation had run its course and had brought Catholicism again to ethical and disciplined behaviour the continued existence of the Reformation became to the Roman Church an inexplicable fact. If it were to be explained then it would have to be in pathological terms along the lines of the physical and mental aberrations of Luther. It is interesting to see that that approach still persists, and just before the visit of the Pope to Germany in 1979 the Roman Catholic Church there published a scurrilous attack upon the sanity and character of Luther.

All this appears to confirm the view that the Roman Catholic appraisal of the Reformation and of contemporary Protestantism is still at bottom the same. In the new ecumenical atmosphere of today this creates a sense of impatience. 'Surely', says a recent writer, 'the Protest is now without point? Has not Catholic truth survived intact despite the painful yet unsuccessful attack of the Reformation? Has not Catholicism responded from the time of Trent on, to call for purification and reform? Has not the council imparted still more vigour to its system and restored it to its genuine fulness and essential Catholicity? If the victims of this great misunderstanding of history still persist, and harden, in their attitude, they only show their rather pathological abnormality'.

But this reveals that the Catholic mind does not understand what Protestantism is all about; that it does not exist merely to protest against the abuses of Roman Catholicism, but primarily to testify to the truth of the Gospel, which the basic doctrines of the Roman Church deny. Protestantism does not live in a negation; it has its own positive system of biblical, evangelical doctrine to affirm, and this doctrine is incompatible with the teaching of the Church of Rome. Yet it is that teaching which Rome cannot and will not discuss or reform. And it is clear that the Second Vatican Council was not called for that purpose, but in order to consider and reform the structure, the order and the administration of the church and make it more effective and relevant to the present age.

We have already seen how the decree of the Second Vatican Council on the Constitution of the church left the doctrinal position of the primacy and infallibility of the Pope exactly where it was at Vatican I. The decree on the principle of the collegiality of bishops, that is, that the pastoral office of the bishop is exercised by divine authority and that the synod of bishops meets to assist the Pope, is in fact nothing new in terms of doctrine. Before the Council of Trent bishops of the Church of Rome had fairly wide powers. At the Council of Trent these were taken away and vested in the curia at Rome, the central office of the Roman Catholic Church. This body tends to be made up almost entirely of Italian priests, bishops, and monsignors. This has led to tensions at times between it and the bishops. The decree on collegiality and the setting up of the synod of bishops in Rome was therefore intended to off-set the power of the Italian curia. But it was breaking no new ground doctrinally when it passed its decree on collegiality. It was merely effecting a redress of the administrative balance in the church and restoring the position that had existed formerly.

Such changes could not and did not affect the doctrinal understanding of episcopal or papal offices in the church, or materially alter the relation between them. Alongside these reforms the whole traditional position was written into the conciliar documents, for example:

> . . . his [the Pope's] definitions, of themselves, and not from the consent of the Church, are justly styled irreformable, for they are pronounced with the assistance of the Holy Spirit, an assistance promised to him in blessed Peter. Therefore they need no approval of others, nor do they allow an appeal to any other judgment . . .

This enabled Pope Paul, when he so chose, on November 16, 1964, to remind the council both in word and deed that the college of bishops acts only with the consent of its head. A few days later he prevented a decision being taken on religious toleration, and in 1966 he proclaimed rules of restriction on the right of bishops to grant dispensations. Only a short time before this the Pope refused to put into effect five decrees of the council as originally scheduled. In 1981 Cardinal Hume went to the Synod of Bishops in Rome with high hopes of pressing upon the Pope the need for reform in areas of discipline such as birth control, which would give the Roman Catholic Church in England the enlightened and more liberal image it is seeking. But he came away empty handed and many of the aspirations fostered by the talk of collegiality at the Second Vatican Council and since, have suffered a set back. The reality of the true situations seems to be dawning upon the Roman Catholic Church itself. Protestants at least ought to show a similar awareness.

What is true of Papalism and episcopacy is also true of other areas dealt with by the Second Vatican Council. We may take the concept of priesthood. In the decree on the Dogmatic Constitution of the church it is declared that the church comprises the whole people of God, clergy and laity alike.

Protestants have long asserted that the church is the company of believers, as Article XIX of the Church of England affirms. There is no radical or essential distinction between ministers and people. The clergy are simply set apart for the purpose of ministering the Word and sacraments. This is a difference of function not of status. The

59

New Testament position is that all believers are priests (Revelation 1:6), for all come to God solely through the mediation and priesthood of the Lord Jesus Christ. There is no order of men set apart to exercise a special priestly office, and act as intermediaries between God and man.

But the Roman Catholic Church has consistently taught that the priesthood of the church is a body of men ordained specially to act as mediators between God and man in the mass. They share, it is said, in a special way in the high priesthood of Christ, in offering his sacrifice in the mass and in dispensing the forgiveness of sins. The powers of Christ as priest and mediator are held and exercised on earth by them, by virtue of their ordination in the apostolic succession. Only those who are so ordained are eligible to exercise this authority and ministry.

It might therefore appear that the Roman Catholic Church in its decree on the Constitution of the church is introducing something which is new and likely to qualify its doctrine of the priesthood, when it affirms that the church consists of the whole people of God, clergy and laity alike. But in fact the doctrine of the priesthood is not affected in any way. It is still only the priest who can officiate at mass and offer what is called the holy sacrifice. It is still only the priest who can pronounce absolution, and they still claim to act as mediators between God and the laity. In the Council's documents the essential difference between the priesthood and the laity is maintained: '. . . they differ from one another in essence not only in degree . . . The ministerial priest, by the sacred power he enjoys, molds and rules the priestly people. Acting in the person of Christ, he brings about the Eucharistic Sacrifice, and offers it to God in the name of all the people'. Though the laity are referred to as priests, or priestly people, yet no one should be misled by this, for the qualitative distinction fundamental to Catholicism, but foreign to Protestantism, between the 'common priesthood' of the people and the 'hierarchical priesthood' of those ordained to the ministry is preserved throughout.

The decree on the Constitution of the Sacred Liturgy did

not make any radical change in doctrine, as many Protestants might have been led to believe from many of the outward changes that have since manifested themselves in the form of the mass and the way it is now conducted. The decree forms the basis for the pastoral renewal of the liturgy. It recommends that there be readings and sermons at all masses, and that Latin should be replaced by the mother tongue in the mass and other sacraments. The ritual may also be adapted to the culture of different countries. However, just before the fourth and last session of the Second Vatican Council the Pope in his own right and in his own words issued the encyclical *Mysterium Fidei*. In this encyclical he stated that all Roman Catholics must hold the doctrine of the mass as it had been enacted and decreed at the Council of Trent, and that no one must think, 'that although a doctrine has been defined once by the Church, it is open to anyone to ignore it or give it an interpretation that whittles away the natural meaning of the words or the accepted sense of the concepts'. He emphasized the traditional doctrine of the mass and that, 'the Church has always offered it not only for the sins, punishments, satisfactions and needs of the faithful still alive, but also for those who have died in Christ but are not yet fully cleansed'. The Pope also insisted upon the dogma of transubstantiation in its proper and traditional sense, and upon the veneration and worship due to the sacrifice, as due to God himself, which was an essential part of the decree of Trent.

Thus the outward changes that we witness in the mass today do not testify to any change of doctrine on the part of the Roman Catholic Church. When a layman reads the epistle dressed in lay clothes and not vested in any way, and when the epistle and the rest of the service is in English and its form resembles that of the new services of the Church of England or the other Protestant churches we must not draw the conclusion that therefore the doctrine of the mass has now changed, and the Church of Rome has now adopted a biblical doctrine of the Lord's Supper. This is not so. The real difference is still there under the new form. In the Church of Rome it is still believed and taught

61

that the priest is offering a real sacrifice for sins, whereas Protestants teach that the Lord's Supper or the Holy Communion is for the continual remembrance of the sacrifice of Christ. A deep difference which remains unchanged since the Reformation.

The absence of doctrinal change in the areas we have examined in the documents of Vatican II is very significant, for the papacy, the priesthood and the mass are three key areas doctrinally for the Roman Catholic Church. They are bound to govern and control most other things. It might have been expected that if there had been any overture to Protestants it could have been detected here. Of course the Second Vatican Council dealt with many other issues of a doctrinal nature such as Revelation and Scripture, and Mary. Some of these will be considered in Chapter 11, in the summary of the remaining differences between Protestantism and Rome. Many other matters dealt with by the council were domestic and adminstrative questions for the Roman Catholic Church, such as the kind of dress to be worn by monks and nuns and the desirability of their participating more fully in pastoral ministry. Such things do not specially concern us. They are simply the response of the Church of Rome to changed social and cultural conditions of the twentieth century, but do not signify any real change which could make us think that the Church of Rome is now different from what it was 400 years ago.

Before we leave the subject of the Second Vatican Council, however, something should be said about the decree on ecumenism. This states that there must be a new relationship to non-Roman Christians, which is to be brought about by a thorough knowledge of one's own faith and of the teaching of the non-Roman Catholic churches, so that the two may be compared. This does not, of course, mean that Rome is making any concessions to Protestantism. It simply means that the Roman Catholic Church is willing to enter into dialogue with non-Roman Catholic churches, on the understanding that she continues to hold fast her faith. This is done in the hope that Protestants and others will recognise the 'fullness' of the Roman Catholic faith and move towards that position as a result of dialogue.

On the part of Rome this is not an unreasonable expectation. It has been evident for some time that the historic Protestant churches have lost the dynamic of Reformation teaching and faith, and have ceased to be controlled by the essential tenets of Protestantism. The growth of biblical liberalism in the last century and this, the spread of Anglo-Catholicism in the Anglican churches, (which has not been without its sympathisers in other denominations), but above all the decay of the vital religion and faith which spring from encounter with the Word of God, which is the reason for the existence of Protestantism, have all contributed to the mood of uncertainty and confusion which has characterised the present age. It is not surprising therefore that the Church of Rome should see in this an opportunity. She could achieve nothing if she remained aloof, but much might be gained if she were prepared to show a willingness to be involved even to a limited extent.

There are already many indications that things might move in that direction. What was happening before the Second Vatican Council and what has happened since have served to show that such a calculation was correct. The movement has all been in a Romeward direction. A tide has been moving through all the Protestant Churches taking them towards a more Catholic understanding of the church, ministry and sacraments. In Methodism and the Free churches there has been a movement towards the acceptance of episcopacy and liturgy. In Anglicanism there has been a movement towards Roman Catholic teaching on eucharistic sacrifice, priesthood, mariolatry and even the papacy. Thus everything leads in a Romeward direction. It would be foolish to pretend that the Church of Rome takes no account of these things. On the contrary it views them as confirmation of the truth of its teaching that the fulness of the faith is to be found only in itself and its own teaching, and the various movements which reflect in a fragmentary way the truth that is found in its wholeness only in the

Roman Church all tend thither. The statements of the Vatican Council can really leave us in no doubt about that:

> . . . the unique Church of Christ . . . constituted and organised in the world as a society, subsists in the Catholic Church, which is governed by the successor of Peter and by the bishops in union with that successor, although many elements of sanctification and of truth can be found outside her visible structure. These elements, however, as gifts properly belonging to the Church of Christ, possess an inner dynamism toward Catholic unity.

Such then is the state of things after Vatican II. The Church of Rome is essentially the same church doctrinally as it was before. Protestants should be under no illusion about this. And, therefore, that Protestantism which understands itself aright and knows the reason why it exists and the Gospel to which it is committed can be no nearer reconciliation with Rome than it was before.

It seems that the two systems run on parallel lines—the one is the antithesis of the other—and therefore however far you project them they will never meet. It is said that when Archbishop Fisher made his historic visit to Rome to meet Pope John XXIII in 1960, the Pope is supposed to have said something about the 'return' of separated brethren. The Archbishop asked him not to use the word *return*—'Your Holiness, none of us can ever go *backwards*. Our two Churches are now running on parallel lines. We must look forward in the hope that one day the lines will converge'. But while parallel lines appear to converge they never really do. And it is the inward logic and constraint, the very rationale, both of Protestantism and Catholicism which will ensure it is realised that they can never meet.

5: The nature of Roman Catholicism

Today, many people in the churches are saying that what unites Christians is greater than what divides them. If this is applied to the various Protestant churches we would agree. But it is now being said of Roman Catholicism as well, and the inference is that we should let the 'secondary' things go and hold onto the essential or primary deposit of truth that is common to both Protestants and Roman Catholics. The division between Protestantism and Roman Catholicism however, goes much deeper than is commonly supposed, and if traced to its source is seen to reach to the foundation of both systems. The whole understanding of the church and salvation is so profoundly different in each case that it defies the simple and straightforward interpretation suggested.

In the Appendix I deal with some of the main differences that remain between the two. It would be a mistake to suppose that these differences are only slight or incidental, and that if we chose to ignore them, then deep down we should still share a common faith and basic agreement upon the Christian religion because we have the Bible and the creeds in common. The differences to which we shall refer are not optional extras at all: they arise out of different understandings of the Christian religion which are diametrically opposed. It is at this level that we must try to grasp the difference between Roman Catholicism and Protestantism. Roman Catholicism is, as Newman said, a different religion. It breathes a different atmosphere, and possesses a different orientation upon the fundamental truths of the Christian religion. The particular differences, with which we shall deal later, are but the outward expression of this fundamental cleavage, which is latent at the deeper level, but little noticed or considered in the present climate of popular ecumenism.

The general lack of comprehension of the problem at this deeper level is illustrated in the subject of the papacy. Many Protestants view the Pope merely as a religious leader, rather like the Archbishop of Canterbury. They fail to appreciate that for the Roman Catholic he has an altogether different status and a quite different 'feel'. When we say that in the Roman Catholic Church the Pope takes the place of Christ and is a kind of surrogate God, the assertion is treated with suspicion and incredulity, as if by saying this we are misrepresenting the teaching of the Roman Catholic Church and being unfair to it. It serves however to reveal the general inability on the part of Protestants to appreciate the real difference, and even to enter sympathetically into the Roman Catholic mind. It is precisely at this level that much well-meaning ecumenism fails because it is unrealistic. In trying to be polite and 'fair' to Roman Catholicism it fails to enter into the real texture of thought of the Catholic mind and remains bound by its own presuppositions. Hence the Pope is a sort of religious leader, much like any other religious leader. Such thinking is both unrealistic and dangerous. It would be truer to say he is a sort of god.

The difficulty for Protestants, in even conceding this understanding of things, is the failure to see how you arrive at that position in the first place. How do you get from a man in the Vatican to some kind of semi-divine being? It is like looking at some plateau high up on a mountain, which to the inexperienced climber seems impossible to reach. But there is a path which he does not see. The Protestant must make some effort to understand Roman Catholicism, and to see how for 500 million people the Pope can become some kind of god on earth. Without that realization he will always misjudge and underestimate the significance of the Roman Catholic religion and the power of the Church.

The reasoning which lies behind Roman Catholicism as the justification for such thinking, is the idea that the Church is the extension or continuation of the earthly life of Christ, the Incarnation. At the Ascension, Christ did not abandon the earth. He remained in the form of the Church. His saying, 'Lo, I am with you always, even unto the end of the world' (Matthew 28:20), is taken literally to mean that his physical presence is with the Church in the form of the Pope and bishops of the Roman Catholic Church. It is through them that Christ is made present in the world today. The Church is the body of Christ, and Christ is its head. The head, it is argued, is part of the body, and in dealing with the body, the Church, we are dealing with the 'total Christ'. The distinction between Christ and the Church is broken down and disappears, not only in practice but in doctrine.

> There is a shifting movement from Christ to the Church, from apostles to bishops, from revelation to dogma, from Gospel to tradition . . . So it is but natural that the attitude of discipleship, submission, obedience that is due to Christ, be applied to the Church, and that Christ's mediatory function pass to the Church, that he who is *Dominus et Magister* be represented by the Church, *Domina et Magistra* and that the one name that is given to men whereby we must be saved, be attributed not only to the Lord, but to his legitimate representative on earth, *Sanctissimus Dominus noster Papa*.[1]

Thus the Church clothes itself with the robes of Christ's majesty, authority and glory, and in the eyes of discerning Protestants commits the ultimate blasphemy. But to the Roman Catholic it is the normal mode of his thinking about the hierarchy and is the guarantee of the actual presence of Christ in the world today.

The implications of all this are clear. In order to come to Christ you must come to the Church. No man comes to the Father in heaven but through the Church, and that means coming to the Father who sits upon the throne of Peter in Rome and in every confessional. Christ is physically present today on earth in the person of the Pope, and as those seeking salvation came to Christ when he was on earth in his own person, so now they must come to Christ through his vicar on earth, and through the bishops, through whom the presence and power of Christ is now mediated.

John XXIII, the most 'ecumenical' of the Popes, wrote in his apostolic letter 'Quotiescumque nobis', 29 June, 1961:

> There is no service rendered properly and acceptably to God and none can come to him, except through Jesus Christ. It is not possible to be united with Christ except in the Church and through the Church, which is his mystic body. It is not indeed possible to belong to the Church, except through the bishops, the successors of the apostles, united to the Supreme Pastor, the successor of Peter.

Thus we have the identification of the Church with Christ, its Head. As the encyclical 'Mystici Corporis' (1943) puts it: 'Christ . . . lives in the Church and by means of her, teaches and governs and communicates holiness', in such a way that through the members of the hierarchy, 'in virtue of that very mandate of the Redeemer, the gifts of the Teacher, King and Priest become everlasting'. The Roman Church, it is claimed, carries out and exercises those three roles of Christ here on earth.

The Teacher

The infallible teaching authority of the Pope, to which we have referred in the documents of both the first and second Vatican Councils, is said to be the manifestation of the presence of Christ in the Church today. As it is unthinkable that Christ, the Son of God, should have been mistaken in what he taught, so it is unthinkable, in the Catholic Church, that the Pope, and the bishops in conjunction with him, should be mistaken in what they teach. Many Protestants view the decree on infallibility of the first Vatican Council of 1870 as a mistake on the part of the Roman Catholic Church, which they believe it would now like to undo, in the cold light of the twentieth century. Such Protestants must think again. Taken in the context of the whole history and development of Catholic doctrine the decree on infallibility was no aberration, but the necessary formulation of what has been latent in the tradition of the Church of Rome.

This means, of course, that Roman Catholics do not understand the Bible as Protestants do. For Protestants the Bible is God's Word to the Church. It stands over the Church to judge its doctrine and cleanse its life. It was through such an independent and objective understanding of the authority of the Bible that the Reformation of the Church, doctrinally and morally, was possible. The Bible for the Roman Catholic is only significant within the context of the tradition and teaching authority of the Church of which it is only a part. The Church, it is argued, preceded the writing of Scripture, selected the books that were to be included in the Bible and set the seal of authenticity upon it. The Church alone interprets and transmits the Christian message to every generation, and that message consists not merely of the Bible but also the unwritten tradition received by the apostles from the lips of Christ and also by dictation from the Holy Spirit, and which constitute a source of revelation equal to that of Scripture. Removed from the living tradition of the Church, the Bible has no meaning. It is the 'dead word', whereas the teaching authority of the Church is called the 'living word'. Bible reading must, therefore, have an entirely different meaning for the Catholic from what it has for the Protestant. This should help to show how the difference of spirit and ethos, which underlies Roman Catholicism, must affect everything it teaches and indeed everything it touches. To say that we have the Bible in common, and yet not to appreciate or understand the approach to the Bible that Roman Catholicism dictates is to fail to grasp the depth of the problem that faces us.

For example, the role of biblical interpretation is reversed in Roman Catholicism. The order is first the dogma then the search for the Scripture texts that may substantiate it. Pius XII in his encyclical '*Humani Generis*' has put clearly what this means. The task of the theologian is to, 'Show how the teachings of the living *magisterium* (teaching authority) are to be found either explicitly or implicitly in holy scripture or divine tradition'.

The teaching of the Fathers and the Church must not be subjected to the judgement of Holy Scripture, but rather we must expound Scripture according to the mind of the Church, which has been made by Christ the Lord the guardian and interpreter of the whole deposit of revealed truth.

This is what the doctrine of the Church as the extension of the Incarnation of Christ means. The Church is inevitably set above the Word of God making it sterile, and ineffective, just as Christ said the Pharisees had by their tradition made the Word of God of none effect. The Bible becomes, in fact the creature of the Church, and the teachings of the Church become irreformable.

The Priest

Here, again, in the function and authority of the priest in the Church of Rome we have an identification of Christ with the Church. In Protestantism we regard the high priestly work of Christ for man's redemption as finished on the cross, where he made, by himself, 'one perfect sacrifice, satisfaction and oblation for the sins of the whole world'. Moreover, we regard the priesthood of Christ as unique and inalienable, ie, it cannot be transmitted to any other. The word used in Hebrews 7:24 is *aparabatos*, which means 'without successor'. In this way it differed from Aaron's priesthood which was passed on to others. Christ's priesthood is 'perfect' (Hebrews 7:28), complete, and peculiar to himself. Because he made a perfect offering for sin 'once for all' he requires no successor and no further sacrifice. The idea that the Christian ministry shares in, and perpetuates, the sacrifice of Christ is alien to the teaching of the New Testament.

However, because the Roman Catholic Church views itself as extending and continuing the work of the incarnate Christ here on earth it sees this work of redemptive sacrifice as going on now through the agency of the priesthood, which has been ordained specially for this task of offering the sacrifice of Christ continually to God the Father for the sins of the world. The priest is described an *alter Christus* (another Christ) and his ordination is supposed to confer on him 'the power to act in virtue of, and in the person of, Christ himself' and thus to offer the same sacrifice which Christ offered on the cross.

The heart of the matter is the idea that the work of Christ cannot be limited to the three short years of his earthly ministry. He must be put in touch with all men everywhere, and this is done through the Pope and the bishops, and the priests whom they ordain. 'The bishop', as an intelligent Roman Catholic layman put it recently, 'gives life. He is officially the life-giver, the giver of Christ's life'. And the priest participates in this ministry by virtue of his ordination at the hands of the bishop. Those who would have life and salvation *must seek it at the hands of the priest*. 'To the priests then, must he have recourse', said Pius XII in 1947, 'whoever wishes to live in Christ', because they are, 'the divine instruments by means of which one shares the supernatural life with the mystical body of Jesus Christ'.

The power to forgive sins and to offer sacrifice for sins is therefore, for Roman Catholics, *now* vested in the priesthood. The priest has the power to make the life of Christ present to men because he alone has the authority to do so. The people cannot do it for themselves. Hence the notion of the priesthood of the people, while it is a reality in Protestantism, does not exist in Roman Catholicism despite the language of the second Vatican Council. The people, the encyclical of Pius XII says, 'representing in no sense the person of the Divine Redeemer, neither being mediators between themselves and God, cannot in any way enjoy sacerdotal power'. This real and unbridgeable distinction between the laity and the priesthood is maintained in Vatican II by the device of calling the so-called priesthood of the people a 'common priesthood' and that of the priests a 'hierarchical priesthood'. It is the same thing as giving everybody a rise and so maintaining the differentials. The people are just as much dependent upon the priest for divine grace now as they were before.. None of the power or authority of the priesthood is diminished and the priests are the sole mediators between God and the people.

The force and significance of what this really means is shown in a Pastoral letter written in 1905 by Johannes Katschtaler, Prince Bishop of Salzburg. Since Vatican II has changed nothing in this respect the principles are still valid:

> Honour the priest because of two inexpressibly high powers with which he is endowed.
>
> I. . . . the Catholic priest has the power to forgive sins . . . God has, as it were, to this end surrendered his omnipotence for this moment to his representative on earth, the duly empowered priest.
>
> Of course, the priest does not possess this altogether wonderful power of himself, but because of his ordination and because he is so empowered through the holy Church . . . Protestant pastors have not the priestly ordination.
>
> II. The priests have the power to consecrate . . . to make present the Body of the Lord with the precious Blood, with his entire Manhood and his Godhead under the form of bread and wine . . . There at Bethlehem Mary bore the divine Child and wrapped him in swaddling clothes: the priest does the same as he lays the Host on the Corporal. Once did Mary bring the divine Child into the world. But, lo! the priest does this not once, but hundreds and thousands of times as often as he celebrates . . . But do they make the Body and Blood of the Lord merely present? No, they sacrifice; they offer the sacrifice to the heavenly Father. It is the same sacrifice that Christ made by shedding his Blood on Calvary . . .

This shows unambiguously what priesthood means in Roman Catholic terms. There is no point in pretending that it means less. The whole rationale of the Roman Catholic Church, which claims that it is the extension of the incarnation, requires it to be so.

The King

Christ's spiritual body, the Church, in its hierarchy of Pope and bishops holds the power of the royal sovereignty of Christ its head. Thus the hierarchy claims the right of government and jurisdiction, the power to rule by command and to bind the conscience. In this way the Church ceases to be obedient to the Lord of the Church and becomes a ruling Church which is indistinguishable from its head and which commands obedience. Protestants detect in this assumption of absolute authority by the Church the usurpation of a spiritual power and prerogative which belong only to God and his Word. It displays a spirit and temper which are not found in the New Testament where none of the apostles speaks in this way. The apostle Paul, for example, is very careful to distinguish between what the Lord had said, which was of divine command, and what he said to the church, which fell into an altogether different category. There is no such confusion between the head and the body as is later witnessed in the Roman Catholic Church. Nor is there any suggestion that the apostles lorded it over the faith and consciences of Christians. Rather they explicitly disowned such dominion and regarded themselves in a different role as 'helpers' or ministers of faith. (2 Corinthians 1:24).

The Roman Catholic Church also considers it right to rule in the temporal affairs of the world since the Church's hierarchy represent, the kingly rule of Christ on earth. It is through the Pope, the bishops and the priests that the sovereignty of Christ is exercised in the affairs of nations and society. Their influence and authority is coterminous with the influence and royal sway of Christ and his kingdom on earth. This rule is extended through the laity whose duty is to enlarge, 'the orbit of the apostolic light of the hierarchy'. Thus wherever a Roman Catholic laymen is placed, at any level of society, he must see it as his duty to extend the influence and authority of the Roman Catholic priests and bishops, and ultimately of course the Pope, for this, it is claimed, is the same as extending the Kingdom of God. This is a very different conception of things from that which the Protestant layman entertains when he talks about praying and working for the coming of God's Kingdom.

The paradox presented by Roman Catholicism of the pomp and splendour associated with the Pope and the dignitaries of the Church, though much reduced since the *aggiornamento* of Pope John the XXIII, creates no difficulty for the Catholic mind once the premise on which it rests is recognised, viz, that the hierarchy are the focus of the rule of Christ on earth. Such ceremony, it is considered, is only the outward expression of the assumption by the Church of the power of him to whom all authority in heaven and earth is given. The Pope becomes 'Lord of Lords and King of Kings', the very titles ascribed to Christ himself in Scripture. He is described as 'Father of Princes and Ruler of the world' at his enthronement. These titles may seem unreal and unbelievable to most Protestants so that they cannot take them seriously or attach much importance to them. But there is no indication that the Church of Rome is ceasing to take them seriously. The whole rationale of its theology of the Church requires that they be given the same validity as the dogma of the infallibility of the Pope. The Church of Rome does believe that it has the right and the authority to rule over the kingdoms of the world.

We see then the supposed justification in the Roman Catholic mind for the authority, the power and the glory which the Church of Rome arrogates to itself. But as Protestants we consider the premise to be mistaken and all the claims which derive from it false. The division between the two systems, Protestantism and Roman Catholocism, is not superficial but fundamental. The claim of the Church of Rome, that it is endued with the authority and power and majesty of Christ, has turned it into a caricature of what the body of Christ ought truly to be. From being the bride of Christ it has become the unfaithful harlot.

6: A Protestant nation

'Those who forget their history end up as slaves in the gutter.' Those words, spoken recently by a politician, remained in my mind because they pin-pointed a real weakness of Protestantism today. One of the principal reasons for the drift in the Protestant churches towards Rome is the neglect of history. We shall not understand ourselves, and we shall certainly not understand the Church of Rome, unless we take the trouble to acquaint ourselves with what has happened in the past.

This is not irrelevant to religion. The Bible views history and religion as intertwined. This is because it speaks of the living God who intervenes in the world. The prophets of Israel reminded them repeatedly of God's saving acts in history. The exodus from Egypt, the crossing of the Red Sea, the entry into Canaan were events they were continually recalling. Without this sense of history they would be without an awareness of God's dealings with them as a people, they would not understand themselves or their relationship with God.

The same must be true for us today. If we believe in a God who acts and intervenes in the affairs of men, and in particular in the affairs of our nation; in a word, if we believe in Divine Providence, we cannot be forgetful of our history or we shall be forgetful of God, we shall despise his mercies and deliverances. 'Praise the Lord, O my soul', says the Psalmist, 'and forget not all his benefits'.

The Basis of our Constitution

The fact that today we are a Protestant nation with a Protestant throne derives from a fundamental principle of the Reformation, which is that individuals and nations must be ruled by the Word of God. At the Diet of Worms in 1521

Luther appealed to the authority of the Bible over his conscience as the reason for rejecting the authority of the Pope and councils, and also for refusing to retract any of his teachings. His words were:

> Unless I am convinced by testimonies of the Scripture, or by evident reason—for I neither believe the Pope nor the Councils alone, since it is clear that they have often erred and contradicted one another—I am overcome by the Scriptures I have quoted, and my conscience is taken captive by the words of God, and I neither can nor will retract anything, since it is neither safe nor right to act against conscience.

What was for Luther at Worms the assertion that the individual conscience must be ruled by the Word of God was later, in 1529 at the Diet of Speiers, taken a step further by the princes and the Reformers. There the principle was extended from the individual to the ruler and the community. The sole authority of the Bible must also govern the conscience of the prince so that it is his right and duty to order things in the nation over which he rules according to the teaching of God's Word. Thus the supremacy of the Pope in spiritual matters was thrown off and the reformation of the church and of the world which had been held back by the intransigence of the hierarchy was made possible.

The English Reformers saw this as the way to reform in England, and while they spoke of the supremacy of the king they showed that it was a supremacy that was qualified by, and subject to, the ultimate authority of God's Word. As Tyndale wrote in *The Obedience of a Christian Man*, 'As God maketh the King head over his realm, even so giveth he him commandment to execute the laws upon all men indifferently. For the law is God's, and not the King's. The King is but a servant, to execute the law of God, and not to rule after his own imagination'. Subjects must obey the monarch, but the monarch in his turn has the overriding duty of obeying the Scriptures.

This is of course essential to the British constitution and the doctrine of the Church of England, in the 39 Articles of Religion, and the Royal Supremacy is still operative today. It is necessary to remind ourselves of the principles upon which it rests.

The Bill of Rights

When over a 100 years later this position was threatened by the efforts of James II to reintroduce the Roman Catholic religion and the authority of the Pope, and to subvert the national church, a Bill of Rights (1689) was passed by Parliament to safeguard the Protestant character of the throne and the Church of England so that the people would continue to be free to worship according to the Protestant faith. The relevant section of that Bill is worth quoting:

> Whereas it hath been found by experience, that it is inconsistent with the safety and welfare of this Protestant kingdom, to be governed by a popish prince, or by any king or queen marrying a papist, the said Lords spiritual and temporal, and Commons do further pray that it be enacted, that all and every person and persons that is, are, or shall be reconciled to, or shall hold communion with, the see or Church of Rome, or shall profess the popish religion, or shall marry a papist, shall be excluded and shall be forever incapable to inherit, possess, or enjoy the Crown and Government of this Realm . . . and in all and every such case the people of these realms shall be, and are hereby absolved of their allegiance.

It had been found by experience, the Bill declared, both ancient and recent, that this arrangement would not work. A Roman Catholic king or queen could not and would not govern in the interests of a Protestant church and nation, because their allegiance and submission had already been given to a power outside the nation, to a power which was fundamentally incompatible with the principles upon which both the church and nation rested, namely, the Pope of Rome.

The experience of the Middle Ages and the Reformation period had shown that a Roman Catholic monarch was the puppet of the papacy. He was the servant of a master who claimed his whole obedience. He occupied his throne by sufferance, and he was expected to hold open the door of his kingdom for the admission of legates, bishops, edicts, bulls and every servant of his foreign master. Not every

English king was Pope-ridden in this way, but that was because they were bad servants and subjects of the Vatican. The worse servant of the Pope the better an English king. That was ancient experience.

More recent experience had proved the same thing. The history of England from the Reformation had been one of intrigues and plots by those inside and outside the nation to bring England back into the orbit of the papacy. These plots culminated in the plans of James II, who became king in 1685, to subvert the Church of England and to raise an army to establish Roman Catholicism once more. He declared an indulgence to all dissenters, but chiefly with a view to facilitating the emergence of the influence and power of the Roman Catholic priesthood. The successful opposition of the English bishops to this measure led to James's downfall and he was succeeded by William of Orange.

William was invited by Parliament to become king to maintain the Protestant throne and church. The men of the Glorious Revolution, as it was called, who invited him were determined that history should not repeat itself. They were resolved to safeguard the rights of the British people to worship according to the Protestant faith of this country, and to be free from foreign intervention in the affairs of the nation. The first essential therefore was to ensure that the sovereign should himself be free. Only a free man can rule over free men. A Roman Catholic king, it had been shown, was not a free man. His conscience was bound by the authority and jurisdiction of the Pope. If the sovereign was to be free to obey his conscience according to God's Word, he could not be a Roman Catholic, nor could he be married to a Roman Catholic for that was almost the same thing. The closeness of the marriage bond would serve to bind the king in much the same way as if he were a Roman Catholic himself.

The main provision of the Bill of Rights, which still stands on the statute book, was to secure the political and religious rights and freedom of the people of this kingdom, and clearly that could not be done unless the king himself were a free man. A puppet would not do; and the Bill of Rights severed once and for all the sinews of the arm that managed the puppet.

The Protestant succession

The Act of Settlement was devised twelve years later when there was a risk of failure in the line of succession to the throne. Like the Bill of Rights it provides for the forfeiture of the crown if the holder of it is reconciled to the see of Rome, or marries a papist. But in addition it also provides, '. . . that whosoever shall hereafter come to the possession of this crown shall join in communion with the Church of England'.

In recent years we have seen attempts made to change the Protestant succession to the throne, particularly with regard to the clauses in the Bill of Rights and the Act of Settlement which forbid the monarch or the heir to the throne to marry a Roman Catholic. But the argument has been taken further and it has been mooted that the sovereign should be free to be a Roman Catholic himself if he so chooses. In July 1980 when it seemed likely that the matter might be debated in the Commons, the *Spectator* carried an editorial entitled 'Don't unsettle the Settlement' which effectively answered this point. It stated:

> The reasons advanced, for altering the Act of Settlement are flimsy. It is argued that the present provision is offensive to Roman Catholics. This is unlikely as far as the great majority of the country's Roman Catholics who are of Irish origin are concerned. Some English and Scottish Roman Catholics, tending to be few in number and rich in estates, may affect to find the Act of Settlement an insult; but they might as well find the established Protestant Church of England or the established Presbyterian Church of Scotland insulting too.
>
> Some say the Act offensively discriminates against Roman Catholics in a way it does not discriminate against Scots, blacks, Jews (*The Times*) or against Muslims, Hindus, devil-worshippers, Mormons or atheists (Lord Boyd-Carpenter) and that therefore "whatever historic justification" (*The Times*) "it is surely wrong to let this provision continue" (Lord Boyd-Carpenter).
>
> But it was Roman Catholics not Scots, blacks, Jews, Muslims,

Hindus, devil-worshippers, Mormons or atheists, who were a constant threat to parliamentary sovereignty and constitutional monarchy. That they are no threat now is in part due to the established Protestant Church and the Protestant Succession. Why, then, run the risk—however slight it may nowadays appear—of subjecting the country to religious upheaval and subversion by letting them in through a side door?

Since the marriage of the Prince of Wales the clamour for change, which came chiefly from the Roman Catholic Church in this country, has died down. But we may be sure that we have not heard the last of the matter, and at some moment when it is regarded as opportune the attack upon the Protestant throne will be renewed. It is a prize the Church of Rome would very much like to win, or if it is itself denied it, then to ensure that it is not the possession of Protestantism either. If ordinary British people are unaware of the importance of the throne remaining Protestant, the Roman Catholic Church is not, and this can be seen in the special significance attached to the state visit of the Queen to the Vatican in 1980, and the way in which it was interpreted as healing the breach of 400 years. 'The Queen', Patrick O'Donovan, the Roman Catholic journalist wrote, 'was in full papal fig. It was glorious black from head to the ground. . .'. The spectacle of a British Queen dressed in black and being received by the Pope must cause Protestants deep anguish. We can only deplore the wrong advice given to Her Majesty. It did not help matters when *The Times* soon afterwards published a picture of the Spanish Queen dressed in white and wearing a mantilla, and explained that such is the privilege of Catholic queens when they are received by the Pope. The significance of black in the case of our own Queen does not escape us. Any humiliation the Queen suffers is suffered by the nation she represents. Yet we have every reason to be proud and grateful for our Protestant faith. Her Majesty's ministers should be careful to see that the monarch of this Protestant nation is never put in a position which reflects adversely upon the honour and the dignity of the faith we profess.

Rome does not expect to increase her influence and power

primarily through conversions. She had made very little headway in this country in that respect. On that basis and by that method England probably will never become a Roman Catholic country. The number of English Roman Catholics remains the same today as it did in the reign of Elizabeth I, about $1^1/_2$ million. The increase, overall, of Roman Catholics arises chiefly from immigration from Ireland and Eastern Europe. The Roman Catholic Church therefore is primarily interested in securing political and diplomatic influence and power. Hence the recent efforts to obtain diplomatic status for the Pope's representative in London as the first step towards the appointment of a nuncio or full papal ambassador to the Court of St James. All these political and diplomatic moves are very important to the Church of Rome and she is not likely to give up her attempt to get the Act of Settlement and the Bill of Rights changed. As Cardinal Manning put it, the Acts of William III are the sole hindrance to the English Crown being openly and avowedly 'reunited to Christendom by submission to the living authority of the Vicar of Jesus Christ'.

The value of the present position

We should therefore value the Protestant establishment of the throne more than we do. We have seen how the Protestant Reformers viewed it as the alternative to the supremacy of the Pope, but more important than this, they saw in it the principle by which the nation could be ruled by the Word of God. The sovereign is bound to the national church and the national church to the sovereign by ties of mutual recognition and responsibility. It is the responsibility of the sovereign to maintain and promote true religion according to the Bible and it is the responsibility of the church's ministers to pray for the sovereign as the chief magistrate and instruct him or her in the principles and doctrines of Scripture.

This relationship is portrayed in the Coronation service, in which the two principal figures are the Sovereign and the Archbishop of Canterbury, representing respectively the authority of the state and the church. The sovereign swares a solemn oath that he will to the utmost of his power maintain the laws of God, and the true profession of the Gospel; that he will to the utmost of his power maintain in the United Kingdom the Protestant Reformed religion established by law. The archbishop requires this oath before the coronation proceeds. Upon the oath being made a Bible is presented to the sovereign, signifying that it is by the authority of conscience, instructed and informed by the supreme authority of the Word of God, that the nation is to be ruled and the church ordered.

The important thing however is that this should be a reality in our society today, and not simply regarded as some relic from the past that survives into the twentieth century as a mere anachronism, for its implications are of immense consequence for us all. For example, one of the first things that derives from this understanding of our constitution is that we do not live in a pluralist society. Progressive journalists and fashionable innovators have been busy for some time telling us that this is so, whether we like it or not. All religions they say should be taught in our schools: the Christian religion is only one amongst many. All moral views stand on an equal footing. No one has a right to judge between them as far as society as a whole is concerned; it is simply a matter of individual preference. Some public bodies such as the BBC feel it is their duty to adopt a stance of moral and religious neutrality. In fact we are not living in a pluralist society, but in a Christian nation. The basis of this is the solemn oath of the coronation service, which commits this nation to the things of the Christian faith, to the laws of God, the true Gospel and the Protestant Reformed religion. If the coronation oath is not to be regarded as a mere charade, an empty television spectacle, all these things must be enacted in our public life. Our national leaders who bear rule in the name of the Queen, must be seen to be committed to maintaining the values and principles that are enshrined in the coronation service.

It is the business of the Church to declare plainly the teachings of the Bible, so that those who rule might be in

82

no doubt as to what God requires and what are the standards of true righteousness. The form and structure of all this is present in the Protestant constitution of the nation. If the will and vision were also present to carry it out that constitution could become a positive force for good and for the regeneration of society.

Rome—a political institution

We should also remember that Rome is not just another church. It is a political as well as a religious system. In this respect it stands apart and is different from every other church. Most statesmen today feel they cannot ignore the power and influence that the Vatican exerts in international affairs. It is estimated that there are 500 million Roman Catholics. The Roman Catholic Church has its bishops and clergy in virtually every country in the world and they are constantly in touch with the Vatican. The Vatican has therefore the most comprehensive and up-to-date political intelligence system in the world where information of all kinds is exchanged. In countries with large Roman Catholic populations it has the power to influence governments and decide elections. We cannot understand the Roman Church or the papacy until we recognise their dual character as both political and religious. The Roman Church is not simply another church like the Presbyterian or Methodist church. The Pope is not merely a religious leader.

The Church of Rome is in fact founded upon a political dogma. It claims that the Pope is a ruler, or more precisely the supreme ruler of the world, the vicegerent of the Eternal King. Cardinal Bellarmine who was the ablest expounder of the papacy put it thus, 'The pontifical supremacy is the fundamental article of the Christian religion'. In other words the Christian religion, according to the Church of Rome, is founded upon this, that the Pope is the first authority, ruler and monarch upon earth.

It is true that not much is being said about this aspect of the papacy at the present time, but that is because the Church of Rome knows when to keep silent and when to speak. However, like everything else in the Roman system it is still there; nothing is revoked or rescinded. The dogma of the spiritual and temporal supremacy of the Pope remains and reveals the dual character of both the papacy and the Church of Rome itself.

The Vatican makes play upon this dual role to confuse opponents. It uses its civil status to promote its spiritual claims, and its spiritual authority to promote its political claims. For example, if objection is made to any recognition of the Pope's spiritual claims it is said that he is not being recognised as a spiritual leader but as a head of state. But if any objection is raised to the political claims of the papacy it is said that the Pope is the head of a church and a religious leader. This deliberate ambiguity surrounded the invitation to the Pope to visit Britain, and will no doubt be used skilfully to allay fears or disarm criticism.

It seems clear that the Church of Rome takes seriously the political claims of the papacy: it is no outworn dogma. The titles ascribed to the Pope are not empty metaphor or hyperbole, but the clear expression of his fundamental sovereignty. As God's appointed representative on earth, he must be the medium for the revelation of the divine will to man and as such he is necessarily the medium under God of all moral truth and of the validity of all political power.

The papacy claims for its ambassadors, not merely equality with other ambassadors but precedence. The papal nuncio is always expected to be the dean of the diplomatic corps. This is a reflection of the fact that the papacy sees itself not merely as a head of state amongst other heads of state, but as the 'Father of princes and kings and Ruler of the world'. When the people of the Republic of Ireland sang of the Pope, 'He's got the whole world in his hand', it was not popular enthusiasm taking over but the sober teaching of the Church of Rome.

Wherever it is at work Rome seeks not only spiritual but political power. Therefore we should resist every attempt made by Rome to get a nuncio or ambassador into this country, and every attempt to change the terms of the Bill of Rights and the Act of Settlement which relate to the Protestant Succession to the throne.

Rome—always the same

The motto of the Roman Catholic Church is '*semper eadem*' ('always the same'). Its long term objects and aims are always the same. It may at different times adopt a different strategy and appear in a different guise in order to achieve those aims, but its purpose and direction are the same. Rome revokes nothing but only adds to that which is there. This is where a great deal of confusion and misunderstanding has arisen amongst Protestants. They say Rome has changed. But they do not listen to what Rome is saying. Rome does not say that she has changed. These are the words of Pope Paul VI on the Second Vatican Council:

> [The full system of Roman Catholic Dogma] is much wider, as everyone knows, and is not questioned or substantially modified by the Council. On the contrary, the Council illustrates, defends and develops it with extremely authoritative explanations full of wisdom, vigour and confidence. It is this doctrinal aspect of the Council we must consider . . . we must never sever the teachings of the Council from the doctrinal heritage of the Church, but on the contrary discern how they find their place there, how they are consistent with it, and how they give it witness, growth, explanation and application. Then, even the doctrinal or normative 'novelties' of the Council appear in their proper proportion and do not create objections to the faithfulness of the Church to its teaching function, but rather acquire the true significance which makes it shine with a superior light.

The claims and aims of the Church of Rome are the same. She pursues then as resolutely now as she did in the past, but with different means and methods according to the different nature of the times. Her aims and intentions with regard to the Protestant throne and the Protestant Church of England are the same today as they were a 100 years ago: the ecumenical and charismatic movements have simply afforded her the opportunity to prosecute her aims unnoticed by very many Protestants. Their wilful neglect of their own teaching and history and that of the Church of Rome means that their vision is impaired. They see only that which is happening in the present and not the whole strategy and plan of campaign. They do not see as they should, in the lineaments of contemporary Roman Catholicism, the same unchanging figure of Rome imperial and Rome apostate, which has neither revoked nor materially altered any of its tenets, but merely left them in abeyance for a more propitious time than the present, when they may again be brought into play.

7: A reformed Church

The English Reformation is often spoken of disparagingly by its enemies as if it were brought about solely by the desire of Henry VIII to divorce his wife and obtain a male heir. This simplistic view overlooks a fundamental truth of history, which is, that popular movements and revolutions of life and thought are not brought about by single events, but by a complex web of ideas and aspirations which precede and lead up to them.

The English Reformation was indeed a revolution which set this country, its religion, culture, commerce and civilization upon a new and different course. Its origin lay not in the desire of the King to obtain an heir, but, if we are to locate it anywhere at all, in the ferment of new teaching and principles of religion which surrounded the person of Martin Luther in Wittenberg. It was the rediscovery of the Bible, and the realization that its teaching stood out in marked contrast to the universally held beliefs of the Church at that time, which caused the Reformation both on the Continent and in England.

It was this rediscovery of the doctrines of the Bible, which have been outlined in chapter 2, that were the driving force behind the Reformation of the English church and nation, and I want now to sketch in their influence and the profound changes they effected.

The first English reformer

Thomas Bilney was one of the first converts of the Reformation in England. He was a Fellow of Trinity Hall, Cambridge, and his conversion came about in a way that illustrates the close connection at the time between renaissance learning and Reformation truth.

In 1516 Erasmus, the great Dutch scholar, produced his

first Greek text of the New Testament with a Latin translation alongside it in separate columns. It was entitled *Novum Instrumentum*, 'The New Instrument'. This book came into the hands of Bilney who read it first out of scholarly interest, but was led by it to a new appreciation of the Gospel. 'At the first reading (as I well remember) I chanced upon this sentence of St Paul (O most sweet and comfortable sentence to my soul!), in 1 Timothy 1, "It is a true saying, and worthy of all men to be embraced, that Christ Jesus came into the world to save sinners; of whom I am the chief".'

Bilney had begun to grasp the doctrine of justification by the free grace of God through faith alone, as opposed to justification by works. It was to lead him to read the Bible with growing faith and understanding.

The importance of Thomas Bilney for the English Reformation is not merely that he was one of the first to be converted, but that he was so effective in helping to convert others too. It was not long before a group of men from the various colleges were meeting night after night at the White Horse Inn to study Erasmus's New Testament. Among these were men who were later to become leaders of the Reformation in England.

Hugh Latimer

The most famous of Bilney's converts was Hugh Latimer, later Bishop of Worcester and the great preacher of the movement. Latimer at that time was one of the chief opponents of the Reformation at Cambridge. When he took his degree of Bachelor of Divinity he was required to give an oration before the University. He took as his subject the writings of Melanchthon, Martin Luther's colleague at Wittenberg, and proceeded to attack them. Bilney who was present could tell from the vehemence of the discourse that Latimer was not wholly convinced of the position he was defending, and surmised that he was probably in the same spiritual confusion he himself had been in.

Afterwards he sought out Latimer and said that he wished to make his confession to him. He used the occasion not only to tell of his sins and spiritual conflicts, but also to relate how he had found peace through the Word of God. This made a profound impression upon Latimer. Sometime later he recalled this incident when preaching his first sermon before the Duchess of Suffolk. 'Bilney . . . desired me, for God's sake, to hear his confession. I did so; and, to say the truth, by his confession I learned more than before in many years'. On another occasion he said, 'Master Bilney, or rather Saint Bilney, . . . was the instrument whereby God called me to knowledge; for I may thank him, next to God, for that knowledge that I have in the Word of God'. And so Latimer also forsook his studies in the medieval theologians and found a new authority in the Bible.

The converts made in Cambridge by Bilney's testimony were to become the human means under God by which the principles and teachings of the Reformation were to spread later in England. These doctrines would sometimes cause, sometimes follow in the wake of, political changes. But here was the true and latent force of the English Reformation. Without these teachings the transformation of the moral and spiritual condition of the Church and nation would not have come about. The notion that Henry VIII brought about the English Reformation seems rather strange when we remember that he wrote a theological treatise against Luther, and was given the title of Defender of the Faith for it by the Pope. The 'Faith' Henry was defending was the traditional teaching of the Church of Rome, and though he separated from the Pope politically, he never ceased to hold to this 'faith' throughout his life.

The rediscovery of Biblical doctrines inspired the English Reformers with a vision of the Church cleansed from error and brought back into conformity with the Word of God. This was something they shared with the Continental Reformers, Luther, Calvin and Zwingli, who all desired to see the national churches set once again upon a Scriptural foundation. The structures of the church had to be changed in order that it should become the vehicle of the true Gospel. It was a formidable task to overturn centuries of usage and custom, and to challenge doctrines imposed by authority, but they were all convinced that such re-ordering of the church and its worship was necessary so that the truth might be manifested.

Aims of the reformers

The Reformers therefore set themselves to achieve three things which would reflect the teaching of the Gospel, and stand as marks or tokens of a true, reformed church of Christ. 1. To remove completely the sacrifice of the mass and put in its place a communion service 'according to Christ's ordinance'; 2. To ensure that the 'pure word of God is preached'; and 3. To make the nature of the ministry conformable with the Gospel.

First, to remove completely the sacrifice of the mass.

All the Reformers were agreed that the sacrifice of the mass was the root of the Roman Catholic religion. If that remained, as Cranmer said, then every other error would grow from it.

The Roman Catholic teaching of the mass is, that the priest offers Christ's sacrifice to the Father, the very same sacrifice that Christ made upon the cross, and by this continual offering of the mass the forgiveness of sins is obtained and applied to every member of the church both living and dead. Only those ordained by the bishops as priests for the special purpose of offering such sacrifice are empowered to perform this act. And because of its importance as the means by which sins are expiated it is the chief function of the ministerial priesthood.

But when the Reformers looked into Scripture they found no sacrifice of the mass. They saw the sacrifice of Christ made upon the cross, but they read that it was finished and complete. They did not find anywhere authority for believing that that sacrifice was to be perpetuated throughout time by a line of cultic priests, through whose acts and works alone the forgiveness of sins was to be made available. In fact they found no mention of priests at all in the ministry of the New Testament Church.

The sacrifice of Christ upon the cross was made once for all and was past, but the benefits of it were available for all time to those who believed. And the means by which those benefits were to be received were faith in the Word of God and the promise of the Gospel. Thus the communication of the grace of God in Jesus Christ came through the preaching of the Word, not through the massing of priests. This was the theological justification for the Reformers' attack upon the sacrifice of the mass.

We must be very clear about this because it is sometimes argued that what the Reformers were contending with were popular or mistaken notions about the mass which were current at the time, and therefore they were not attacking the real teaching of the mass sacrifice. But they were perfectly clear about what they were doing. They were not attacking false or mistaken ideas about the mass. They were rejecting the very same doctrine that is taught and preached in the Church of Rome today. That was for them the fundamental error. The sacrifice of Christ for sins is past and finished. It is not to be re-enacted and perpetuated by priests but proclaimed by preachers.

Archbishop Cranmer considered this to be one of the 'principal points wherein the papists vary from the truth of God's word':

> They say they offer Christ every day for remission of sin, and distribute by their masses the merits of Christs's passion. But the prophets, apostles, and evangelists, do say that Christ himself in his own person made a sacrifice for our sins upon the cross . . . and so did never no priest, man, nor creature, but he, nor he did the same never more than once. And the benefit hereof is in no man's power to give unto any other, but every man must receive it at Christ's hands himself, by his own faith and belief.[1]

Thus the first and main task of the Reformers was to get rid of the sacrifice of the mass altogether and restore the Holy Communion service in its Scriptural simplicity as a sacrament but not a sacrifice; as a remembrance of the true sacrifice of Christ upon the cross, but not itself an offering for sins. As Bishop Hooper, another of the Protestant martyrs put it, 'I believe that the holy Supper of the Lord is not a sacrifice, but only a remembrance, a commemoration of this holy sacrifice of Jesus Christ . . . and therefore ought the Mass to be abolished, and the holy Supper of the Lord to be restored and set in his perfection again'.

The rejection of the mass and the restoration of the sacrament of the Lord's Supper was the great achievement of all the Reformation churches, and in particular the Church of England, as the Prayer Book service shows. The badge or mark of a true, reformed church is that the sacrament of the Holy Communion is administered 'according to Christ's ordinance', that is, as he has commanded and determined it should be done in Scripture. We are, in these days, in great danger of losing that mark of truth and slipping back into error. The new 'eucharistic' services indicate a departure from biblical simplicity and a return to the doctrine of the mass. To many ordinary people they are indistinguishable from the new Roman Catholic mass in English. There is also the assertion of the International Commission of Anglican and Roman Catholic theologians, set up to study amongst other things the doctrine of these services, that they have reached agreement on this subject. We have seen how the Roman Catholic doctrine of the mass has not changed. It must therefore be that the doctrine of some Anglican theologians has changed. The Church of England is in imminent danger of losing its Reformation heritage, of abolishing the sacrament of Holy Communion and setting up again a mass that is in all important respects indistinguishable from that of the Church of Rome.

Secondly, to ensure that the 'pure word of God is preached'.

The work of preaching was of primary importance to the Reformers for they intended that it should replace the priestly work of offering the sacrifice of the mass. They thus turned the Roman Catholic system upside down. The forgiveness of sins came to men and women when they believed in Christ, when they trusted in him and were 'justified by faith'. Faith was quickened by the Word of God, principally through preaching. Thus, as Latimer said, the office of preaching was the office of salvation. Take away preaching and you take away salvation.

> I told you before of the *scala coeli*, the ladder of heaven; I
> would you should not forget it. The steps thereof are set forth
> in the tenth to the Romans. The first is preaching, then hearing,
> then believing, and last of all salvation. *Scala coeli* is a preaching
> matter, I tell you, and not a massing matter. God's instrument
> of salvation is preaching.

Nothing could be plainer. Christ had told his disciples to
go into all the world and preach the Gospel, not mass it.
Yet the Church of Rome had made the principal work of
her ministry the mass, and preaching had fallen into decay.
Thus a revolution, not less, was needed to topple this system and replace the mass with a preaching ministry directed
at the hearts and minds of the people. The Word offered
salvation, faith applied it to the heart and the sacrament
confirmed and assured faith.

Preaching is therefore central to Protestantism, but not
just any sort of preaching. It must be the 'pure Word of
God'. By the expression 'pure Word of God' the Reformers
intended to convey the idea of biblical preaching based
upon its own principles of interpretation and unmixed with
human tradition or philosophy. The Bible is not the product
of human thought. It is not man's discovery of God, but
God's revelation to man. It can, therefore, only be understood in terms of itself, and in the light of the Holy Spirit's
teaching. He is the true doctor or teacher of the church and
of the individual believer, not the Pope. The Bible is its
own interpreter and is to be understood, as Latimer said,
by the collation and comparison of its parts. Spiritual things
must be compared with spiritual. What is obscure in one
part of Scripture will be made clear by another. That was
how the doctrine of justification by faith itself had been
revealed to Luther and others. Thus the business of preaching is not to declare one's own ideas, theories or opinions
about religion and the Bible, but to 'open Scripture', to
declare the message which the Bible itself has to teach, and
the Gospel which God himself has revealed in his Word.
When this is done faithfully and responsibly the 'pure word
of God is preached' in the Church.

By this means souls are saved, believers are strengthened

and the Church of Christ is established and built upon the doctrine of the apostles and prophets, Christ Jesus himself being the chief corner stone. Where the pure Word is not preached you may have religion, but it will be counterfeit religion. Error, superstition, and ignorance of God will spread. Men will become enslaved spiritually, and the Church will reflect the demonic structures of an anti-Christian system although outwardly it professes the name of Christ. There is no remedy for this but to ensure that the pure Word of God is preached.

William Tyndale who translated the Bible into strong, clear and beautiful English as an essential condition to setting the Word of God free for the English people, also recognised the great need of preachers who would set forth the doctrines of Scripture. With the other Reformers he understood that such preaching was the office of salvation. The universities and schools which had formerly trained the clergy had clouded the issues with human tradition and philosophy, so that the Scripture was, as he said, 'locked up with false expositions and with false principles of natural philosophy'. He sought to outline the true teachings of the Bible in the introductions to the books of the Bible which he wrote for the ordinary reader. But this was really the work of the ministry. His prayer, which we need to use today, was, 'The Lord of all mercy send us preachers with power, that is to say, true expounders of the Word of God'.

It is the decline of preaching of that sort, and the neglect of the principles that underlie it, which are the cause of the radical weakness of Protestantism today. But more seriously it has caused the decline of the church, for a true church is to be found only where the pure Word of God is preached and the sacraments administered according to Christ's ordinance.

Thirdly, succession in the truth, or making the ministry conformable to the Gospel.

The true apostolic succession is a succession in the Gospel. The position of the church today, whether it is in truth or error, can be determined by whether or not it is faithful to Scripture and preaches the same Gospel that we find in the New Testament.

The position of the Church of Rome is quite different from this. There it is contended that the true church is to be found where there is a tactual succession of bishops, an historical line of clergy stretching back in theory to the apostles. This they maintain is the mark of the true church. Identity of doctrine between the church of the New Testament and the church today is not expected or looked for. With tradition and the teaching authority of the church there is a development of doctrine, which means that doctrines can emerge which are not found in Scripture, like the dogma of the bodily assumption of the Virgin Mary. The Roman Catholic is told that they are true because they are taught by those who are in direct lineal descent from the apostles. It is rather like the evolutionary theory of the descent of man from some primitive protozoa. Direct proof is out of the question: there is no resemblance between the two. The argument rests upon a supposed lineal descent, as speculative one might conclude in the one case as the other.

The Protestant case rests upon identity of doctrine between the teaching of the apostles in the New Testament and the church today. Where you have that you have a true church. Truth does not change with the passage of time. It is the same Gospel which is the power of God unto salvation now as then.

We find this principle present in Scripture itself. Paul is very jealous of the Gospel which he preaches. It must, he insists, be at all times and in all places the same Gospel. He is not ashamed to preach the same Gospel to all men, Jews and Greeks. He warns against change and the perversion of the Gospel, against substitute gospels which were being introduced by Judaizers and those who were corrupting the Word of God with heathen philosophies. 'Let no man rob you [of the Gospel] through philosophy and vain deceit, after the tradition of men, after the rudiments of the world, and not after Christ'. The test by which the churches were to decide what was true was to compare everything with the Gospel Paul had preached to them in the beginning. The primitive Gospel was the standard. 'To write the same things to you, to me indeed is not grievous, but for you it is safe' (Philippians 3:1).

Novelty is what the world seeks because it is dissatisfied, empty and restless. The same, unchanged Gospel is the delight of the believer and the church because it is the source of lasting and deep satisfaction. Paul admonishes the Christians at Corinth to stand firm in the Gospel which he had preached to them at the first, (1 Corinthians 15:1), and solemnly declares to the Galatians that though we ourselves, the apostles, or an angel from heaven should preach to them 'any other Gospel than that which we have preached, let him be accursed' (Galatians 1:8). The true test of authenticity of the Gospel is not the source from which it comes, however unimpeachable, but the identity of the message with that which was preached at the first.

Thus the Reformers were right in the stance that they took over against the Church of Rome. Luther interpreted 'apostolic succession' as a succession of doctrine, not of office, ('The Gospel is the only succession') and he recognised only one essential ministry of the church, that of preaching and administering the sacraments. The ministry he held to be the gift of God to the church, that by its exercise faith might be created in people. 'In order that we might obtain faith', ran Article V of the 1531 version of the Augsburg Confession, 'the ministry of teaching the Gospel and ministering the sacraments has been instituted'.

The doctrine of the Church of England followed a similar pattern. 'The Anglican Reformers', wrote Norman Sykes, 'laid great stress upon the reform of the church in order to ensure purity and soundness of doctrine, "the most precious jewel of the Gospel" as Dunham described it, "which is to be redeemed (if need be) with the loss of all outward things" '. The form of government of the church, whether by bishops or presbyters, was in the eyes of all the Reformers secondary to the great concern for faithfulness to the truth of God's Word. Succession of 'place or person' (bishops) was with them of no value if the succession of the

Gospel were lost, if the church ended up preaching a Gospel which was not identical with that of Scripture.

Bishop Jewel, the great Anglican apologist, stated against Harding his Roman Catholic opponent. 'Succession is the chief way for any Christian man to avoid Antichrist, I grant you, if you mean the succession of doctrine'. And again, 'God's grace is promised to a good mind, and to one that feareth God, not unto sees and successions [of bishops]'. For Jewel the touchstone for episcopacy, as for all else in the church, is soundness of doctrine and the faithful conduct of the work of an evangelist. If episcopacy failed in these it failed altogether, and the claim to lineal descent was an empty boast.

Today the subject of bishops is invested with too much importance when it is claimed that they are essential to the church. People are brow beaten and cajoled in ecumenical discussion and schemes for unity into surrendering to this Catholic doctrine of ministry at any price, even the price of doctrinal compromise and departure from evangelical truth. Such exaggerated claims for episcopacy resemble the legalism which our Lord condemned in the Pharisees when they claimed orthodoxy because they said they were the true, lineal descendents of Abraham. If they were the children of Abraham, he said, then they would do the works of Abraham, but since they were not like him in spiritual character their claim to blood relationship and genealogical descent was of little consequence. By their deeds they showed that they were the children of the devil not the children of Abraham.

If bishops are the successors of the apostles they will teach the same doctrines as the apostles. Their Gospel will be identical with that of Paul, and they will not erect a new legalism of works, which is in all respects like the legalism that Paul fought against in order to establish the Gospel of free grace. They will not preach the necessity of priestly sacrifice and priestly mediation. If they do then we shall know them by their fruits, that they are not the true successors of the apostles, but ravening wolves in sheeps' clothing. Claiming to be the true shepherds of the flock of Christ they are really despoilers of it.

Bishops in themselves are no guarantee of the true church. A church may have bishops and yet become apostate and distort the faith of the New Testament, as the church did in the Middle Ages and as the Church of Rome does today. Instead of seeking reunion of the whole of Christendom on the basis of episcopacy and the so-called apostolic succession we should be seeking unity in the truth of the Gospel. Only in doctrinal succession shall we find the marks of a true church, and the ministry, whatever form it takes, is subordinate to that consideration.

We have cause to thank God that in this country we have a church, which has been reformed by the rediscovery of biblical doctrine and that great movement of the Spirit of God which took place 400 years ago; by men who were dedicated to carrying through that reform in the church even to the extent of laying down their lives for it. The Church of England is established upon sound principles and theology, but we cannot take it for granted nor presume upon it for the future. This basis has already been obscured by a resurgence of error, and by infatuation on the part of many of its clergy with the Roman Catholic system. The foundation still remains, the marks of a true church are still to be found in the formularies and official teaching of the Church of England, and if the will were present to restore these things it could still be done. But unless Protestants are prepared to act to save the national church it may soon be too late. Already the foundations themselves are being sapped and undermined. How near we are to losing altogether the marks of a true church is something of which most people seem to be unaware. But the danger is very real as the next chapter will show.

8: Decline and fall?

We have seen how the marks of a true church were brought to light by the rediscovery of the Bible, and established in the Protestant Churches by the Reformation of the sixteenth century. Today the tide is flowing the opposite way. We are experiencing a tendency of thought which moves in the direction of unprotestantising those churches and obliterating the distinctive biblical marks of the church. This has taken place in two areas in particular, in liturgy and worship, and in doctrine.

Liturgy and Worship

In those Protestant Churches which use set forms of service, like the Church of England and the Methodist Church, new forms have been introduced. The Holy Communion service is really the most important one, for it was that service which was carefully revised to exclude the sacrifice of the mass. If a tendency to revert to the teachings and practice of the Church of Rome is taking place it is most likely to show itself here.

For very many years the Anglo-Catholic party in the Church of England tried to get the Prayer Book altered in a Catholic direction but failed. The most notable failure was the rejection of the revised Prayer Book by Parliament in 1928 and again in 1929. That book was rejected principally because of the changes proposed in the Holy Communion service, which would have reintroduced certain ideas and practices which had been rejected at the Reformation. It was proposed to have prayers for the dead. But if we are justified by faith we do not need such prayers. If we believe that Christians who die have departed to be 'with Christ which is far better' why do we need to pray for them? This is a change which is unnecessary and, however

99

small, is a step in the direction of the Church of Rome and its teaching about purgatory and the need to pray for the repose of the souls of the faithful departed.

There was also the desire to introduce some sort of prayer for the bread and the wine, which would suggest that something had been done to them, and that some kind of change had taken place. The only prayer in the Prayer book service was for the people who were to receive the sacrament that they might receive it aright. 'Grant that *we* receiving these thy creatures of bread and wine may be partakers of His most precious body and blood . . .'

But the new prayer was a prayer for the elements that God would bless and sanctify them, that '*they* may be unto us his body and blood'. The change in the words might appear very small, but the difference doctrinally was very great, for it leads onto the understanding that some change, whatever it might be, has now taken place in the bread and the wine by virtue of the prayer the priest has offered over them, and that therefore they are in themselves truly the body and blood of Christ. There was nothing of this in the old service. We can see how the proposed change moves closer to the Roman Catholic ideal and begins to magnify the role of the clergyman as doing something mystical, or even magical, with the elements.

Then there was the attempt to bring back into the prayer of consecration, when the bread and the wine are set apart for communion, the idea of offering. This was quite absent from the Prayer Book. However allusional the idea of offering or sacrifice might be, it would be a foothold for that concept in the prayer which the priest said, and could be invested with the notion of priestly sacrifice. This alone was the explanation of the suggested change, for otherwise there was no reason to alter the prayer at all. It could have been left in the form in which it had served the Church for 400 years.

Finally there was the proposal to reserve the sacrament for the communion of the sick. But to reserve the sacrament suggests that something special inheres in the bread and wine after the communion service is over. The Articles of the Church stated specifically that Christ had not commanded the sacrament to be reserved, and the aim of the Reformers was to administer the sacraments according to the ordinance of Christ.

It was argued that reservation would facilitate the communion of the sick. But it had not been found necessary to do this before, and it could be argued that it was only the growing preoccupation with 'sacramentalism' that was making it necessary then. The Prayer Book stated clearly that where it was impossible for the curate to administer the sacrament to the sick they were still able spiritually to feed upon Christ.

The rejection of these proposals, which would have meant a definite movement of the national church in the direction of the Church of Rome, led to a hiatus. Many of the clergy were not prepared to accept the decision of Parliament. The bishops made it clear that they would not proceed against any clergyman who used the new services, and so for forty years the 1928 service of Holy Communion was used illegally in many parishes.

More recently we have had new services, under the provision of the Worship and Doctrine measure, by which Parliament without giving up its authority has granted the Church of England a degree of freedom to devise new services. Thus we have had Series I, II, III, and more recently Rite A and the Alternative Service Book published in 1980. These services incorporate the main changes that were sought in 1928, and so the Church of England has succeeded in establishing a half-way house between the truly reformed service of Holy Communion in its official Prayer Book and the Mass of the Church of Rome.

The main difference, however, between the 1928 situation and that of today is that there has been liturgical change in other churches too, and in particular in the Church of Rome. The Roman Catholic mass has been put into English, and is now very similar in shape and character to the Eucharist of the Alternative Service Book. The modern rites are very flexible; prayers and readings can be omitted and changed by the local minister and congregation, but the basic structure on which there has been cooperation and agreement by liturgical experts from all the churches shows a remarkable underlying unity. This, it is intended, will facilitate movement between the churches and enable doctrinal differences gradually to disappear from view. As I write, the Archbishop of Canterbury has celebrated the Anglican Eucharist in the Roman Catholic Cathedral in Malines. It is his hope that he will, in the not too distant future, celebrate Mass in a Roman Catholic Church. Judging by the way things are going this does not seem to be an unreasonable expectation. But it will mean the disappearance from amongst us of one of the principal marks of a true church, which the Reformation established, and for which the Reformers considered it was important enough to die. Before we take that final step across the divide, or rather allow ourselves unthinkingly to be swept over it and our Reformation heritage taken away, we might at least reflect on what is involved. As a result of that we may consider that we have already gone too far.

Joint international talks between the Church of Rome and the Anglican Communion began as a result of Archbishop Michael Ramsey's visit to the Vatican in 1966. This in turn led to the setting up of a doctrinal commission known as the Anglican/Roman Catholic International Commission (ARCIC), to explore the controversial questions of the eucharist, the ministry and authority in the church. The first report on the eucharist, which was termed an 'agreed statement', was published in 1971. Since then similar reports have been published on the ministry (1973), and authority (1975). In 1979 a small booklet entitled *Elucidations* appeared from the commission in response to criticisms which had been made of the earlier 'agreed statements'.

The significance of these 'agreed statements' is far-reaching and has implications, not only for the churches directly involved, but for all the churches of Britain. The Church of England stands in the Reformation tradition, and if it can be said that agreement has been reached, and that there remain no material doctrinal differences between it and the

Church of Rome, then this will be regarded as a break-through. Where the Church of England leads, other ecumenically interested churches will be ready to follow. The really important achievement will be that the divide between the Church of Rome and the Protestant Churches will, in principle, have been overcome and the effects of the Reformation neutralised. In no other area has ecumenical dialogue come so close to realising this goal.

It is essential therefore that we understand what these statements are about and exactly how it is claimed that agreement has been arrived at. The areas chosen by the Commission for its theological exploration are the areas where the Reformers believed the marks of a true church must be established: the mass or the Holy Communion; a sacrificing priesthood or ministers of the Word and sacraments; the authority of Scripture alone or of Scripture and tradition and the teaching office of the Pope.

The Statement on the Eucharist (1971)

This statement seeks to reconcile the difference between the concept of the Holy Communion as the remembrance, or commemoration of the sacrifice of Christ which is past, with the idea of the mass as a perpetual sacrifice of Christ by the priesthood, by arguing that remembrance (the Greek word used in the New Testament is *anamnesis*), means actually making the sacrifice of Calvary *present* today in every such service. This subtle device for reintroducing the central concept of the mass is not of course new. The Reformers were aware of it and warned against it, especially in *The Book of Homilies*, 'We must take heed, lest of the memory, it (the sacrament) be made a sacrifice'.

This argument must be rejected because there is no ground for it in Scripture. The only meaning of the word 'remembrance' (*anamnesis*) in the New Testament is 'calling to mind', or 'recollection'. It does not mean what the authors of the report want it to mean, viz, an actual making present of the sacrifice of Christ, in order that it may then be said that the priest makes an offering of it to God. In Scriptural terms there is no room in the Holy Communion service for that understanding of 'eucharistic sacrifice', but only for believing and thankful remembrance of Christ's death for us upon the cross.

It must also be rejected because it is contrary to reason. An event which has happened in the past cannot be made present. This would be to deny its character as an event, ie, an historical happening, a specific point in the time-space continuum. It is not good sense to talk like this, and what is not good sense is not good theology either. The sacrifice of the cross took place in time, in history, and it cannot be arrested and perpetuated in this way. 'It is finished' were the words of our Lord, when he gave up his spirit to God, and they are the only fitting way in which we can speak of his sacrifice. There is no way in which that sacrifice can be *made present*, but its benefits are available to all who believe the Gospel of which the sacrament of Holy Communion is an expression. More than this we do not need, nor should we desire. More than this can only serve to obscure what is necessary.

Finally, we must reject it because the Church of England itself has never taught such a thing.

Archbishop Cranmer wrote:

When I say and repeat many times in my book [on the Lord's Supper] that the body of Christ is present in them that worthily receive the sacrament . . . I mean . . . that the force, the grace, the virtue, and benefit of Christ's body that was crucified for us and of his blood that was shed for us be really and effectually present with all them that duly receive the sacrament.

Dean Aldrich wrote:

It is evident, that since the body broken and blood shed neither do nor can now really exist, they neither can be really present, nor literally eaten or drank; nor can we really receive them, but only the benefits purchased by them.

Archdeacon Waterland, one of the greatest divines of the Church of England, wrote:

We do not say that Christ's death, or Christ's crucifixion, is now *present*; we know it is *past*: but the *benefits* remain; and while we remember one as past, we call to mind or keep in mind, the other also as present.

Thus by a tendentious use of the word remembrance (*anamnesis*), which many people will fail to grasp or not notice, the commission proposes to reintroduce into the Church of England the notion of the sacrifice of the mass and the associated idea of a real presence in the elements. There have been those in the Church of England who have maintained these views in the past and do so today. But it has never been the official doctrine of the Church of England. Formal agreement between the Church of Rome and the Church of England on the basis of the 'agreed statements' would make it so. It would mean that on this vital issue the two churches were agreed, and that could only mean that the Roman doctrine of the mass had been effectively adopted by the Church of England.

The Statement on Ministry (1973)

We have already seen how there is a fundamental difference between the Roman Catholic and Protestant views of ministry. Protestantism regards the ministry as the proclamation of what God has done once for all in the life, death and resurrection of Jesus Christ. The Catholic view of ministry is that the priest again recapitulates, performs and re-enacts what Christ has done, so that he becomes in his office as priest 'another Christ'. The difference put here starkly and simply is the basis of the historic division in Christendom. It can be traced throughout the whole theology of Catholicism and Protestantism. It is the reason why Protestantism is a theology of the Word—the proclamation of a finished work; and Catholicism is the theology of the mass—a work which is never done and never complete.

It should be clear even from a cursory reading of the New Testament which of these two conceptions of ministry has the justification and support of Scripture. The risen Christ commissions his apostles to go into all the world and preach the Gospel to every creature. Now that Christ's work is complete, they are to go and proclaim what God has done in Christ:

Then opened he their understanding, that they might understand the scriptures, and said unto them, Thus it is written and thus it behoved Christ to suffer, and to rise from the dead the third day, and that repentance and remission of sins should be preached in his name among all nations, beginning at Jerusalem. And ye are witnesses of these things. (Luke 24:45–48)

As witnesses they were to declare the things which God had done in Christ for man's salvation. This is exactly what the apostles did. Peter and John declared before the Council of the Jews:

Him hath God exalted to his right hand to be a prince and Saviour, for to give repentance to Israel, and forgiveness of sins. And we are witnesses of these things. (Acts 5:31, 32)

And Paul preaching in Antioch of Pisidia said:

Be it known unto you, men and brethren, that through this man is preached unto you the forgiveness of sins. And by him all that believe are justified from all things, from which ye could not be justified by the law of Moses. (Acts 13:38, 39)

This is the pattern of apostolic ministry, of apostolic proclamation. This is the Word committed to the church. It is the preaching of this Word which is the ministry of reconciliation (2 Corinthians 5:18). Even the Lord's Supper is seen in relation to this primacy of the Word and is another dimension of what is essentially the same activity of proclaiming the finished work of Christ:

For as often as ye eat this bread and drink this cup ye do show [the word used *katangellete* is the same as that for proclaiming the Gospel] the Lord's death till he come. (1 Corinthians 12:26)

The Roman Catholic view of ministry, however, is the very opposite of this. It views the work of Christ not as completed and finished and now simply to be proclaimed by the church, but as needing to be continually re-enacted and perpetuated, by a succession of priests set apart exclusively for that purpose. Thus the work of the ministry is not to declare what has been done once for all for man's redemption, but to effect that redemption now by the sacrificial work of the priesthood.

Between these two conceptions of ministry there is no common ground. The difference is so great that, as Newman said, it constitutes the Roman Catholic faith as a different religion altogether from Protestantism. Yet it is the purpose of the commission to bring these two things together. How can such a thing be done? The answer is to be found in paragraph 13 of the agreed statement on ministry:

Despite the fact that in the New Testament ministers are never called 'priests' (hiereus) Christians came to see the priestly role of Christ reflected in these ministers and used priestly terms in describing them. Because the eucharist is the memorial of the sacrifice of Christ, the action of the presiding minister in reciting again the words of Christ at the Last Supper and distributing to the assembly the holy gifts is seen to stand in a sacramental relation to what Christ himself did in offering his own sacrifice.

This kind of argument, which is characteristic of contemporary ecumenical statements, moves easily and quickly from Scripture to tradition and back again. In the same sentence, in which it is acknowledged that the New Testament never speaks of ministers in a sacerdotal (priestly), sense at all, it goes on to assert that Christians have seen this type of priesthood reflected in the function of their ministers. Having established this understanding of ministry simply by asserting it is so, ie, that the 'priesthood' of the church bears some relation to the priesthood of Christ, it moves on, as we might expect, to argue that the 'celebration of the eucharist' is the most significant and central work of the priesthood, indeed, that, from which the Roman Catholic conception of the ministry derives its rationale:

So it is because the eucharist is central in the church's life that the *essential* nature of the Christian ministry, however this may be expressed, is most clearly seen in its celebration. . . . [My italics]

But by now we have wandered quite away from the New Testament and are in the realm of Roman Catholic orthodoxy. All this is based, not upon Scripture, but upon 'what Christians came to see' in the ministry, in other words upon tradition. The fact is that this assumption about the relation of the Christian ministry to the priesthood of Christ is not biblical at all, yet it is imported into this document despite its claim in the preamble to being biblical. Once it is written into the 'agreed statement', however, it serves to give the Roman Catholic understanding of ministry and priesthood an entrenched position.

Thus the report on ministry, far from being a tentative and uncontroversial exploration of the common ground between the two churches, is a bold attempt to incorporate the traditional Roman Catholic teaching on priesthood.

The Statement on Authority in the Church (1975)

The Protestant position is that there is only one source of authority in the church in all matters of faith, and that is the Bible. Article VI of the Church of England reads:

> Holy Scripture containeth all things necessary to salvation: so that whatsoever is not read therein, nor may be proved thereby, is not to be required of any man, that it should be believed as an article of the Faith, or be thought requisite or necessary to salvation.

The report seeks to qualify this position and introduce other sources of authority by putting the creeds, the Fathers, and the unwritten tradition of the church alongside Scripture. It even tries to suggest that this is already the position of the Church of England. 'In both our traditions the appeal to Scripture, to the creeds, to the Fathers and to the definitions of the early councils of the Church is regarded as basic and normative' (see paragraph 18).

But this simply will not do. Though such statements of belief as the creeds are valued they are nowhere put alongside Scripture as sources of authority. Such a position is incompatible with the plain teaching of the Articles which state that even the creeds are only to be 'received and believed' because they may be proved by most certain warrant of Holy Scripture. Everything therefore relating to the faith of the Church must be proved by Holy Scripture, and that shows conclusively that there is only one source of authority in these matters.

But the statement clearly seeks a great deal more. It

examines not only the role of tradition but also that of the bishops as 'guardians of the truth' in the church, and the place of the Pope, who, by the exercise of *episcope* (oversight) over the whole church, is said to 'promote Christian fellowship in faithfulness to the teaching of the apostles' (paragraph 12), and to maintain 'the whole church in the truth' (paragraph 17).

But if this is the role of the papacy, why has it failed so signally in the past? And why is there such a marked disparity between the teaching of the Church of Rome and the teaching of the apostles in the New Testament? Is not the papacy itself the source of all these unscriptural doctrines, such as, purgatory, indulgences, mariolatry, the sacrifice of the mass, the infallibility of the Pope, and so forth? Are we not now being asked to trust the poacher to be the gamekeeper?

The commission seems to be conscious of the fact that at this point it is on rather insecure ground. It does no more than sketch in these possibilities regarding the role of the papacy in any united church, and defers a fuller discussion until later.

The final revision of the statement on authority has now been completed, as was mentioned earlier, and at the time of writing its contents have not been officially disclosed. The careful timing of the publication might suggest that it has something very important to reveal. Already the joint chairmen of the commission, Bishop McAdoo and Bishop Butler, Anglican and Roman Catholic respectively, have been reported in the Roman Catholic press as saying that they do not regard infallibility as a problem. Both sides are agreed that infallibility is God's gift to the church and that a Pope in general council is capable of making infallible decrees.

This completely subverts the Reformation position. Luther's rejection of Popes and councils, because they are human authorities and can err, is written into all the Protestant Confessions:

General Councils . . . forasmuch as they be an assembly of

men, whereof all be not governed by the Spirit and Word of God . . . may err, and sometimes have erred, even in things pertaining unto God. Wherefore things ordained by them, as necessary to salvation, have neither strength nor authority, unless it may be declared that they be taken out of Holy Scripture. (Article XXI)

If the position of the commission were officially adopted, it would represent not merely a breach with the Reformation on this one point, but the undoing of it altogether, because it would remove the essential safeguard in matters of faith, which is the authority of Scripture alone. Without that to anchor the church in reality, doctrinally, the Church of England, and any other Protestant churches which join it, would be free to launch itself into space, as the Church of Rome has already done.

9: Papal triumphalism

In view of the ecumenical developments discussed in chapter 8, a visit by the Pope to Britain will be of considerable significance for the Protestant churches of Britain, and in particular for the Church of England. It could lead to radical changes in the character of the national church, which would have repercussions on the religious and civil life of this country. I shall try in the later part of this chapter to draw out the ecumenical implications of such a visit. But first I shall deal with two other aspects of the proposed visit, the historical and the constitutional.

The historical dimension

A visit by a Pope to Britain would be a historic occasion, for no other Pope has ever set foot in this country before. That is largely because Popes have not in the past travelled far from Rome, but more particularly since the Reformation it would have been unthinkable that a Pope should visit Britain. A visit of this nature therefore raises a number of historical questions. These are not matters of mere academic interest and best forgotten about, they are questions which are important for us today and determine the nature of any relationship between the papacy and this country. We ought really to know the views of the Pope himself on these matters before he sets foot in Britain.

First, he should tell us how he regards the bull of his predecessor Pius V entitled *Regnans in excelsis*, which excommunicated Elizabeth I and all her subjects who were loyal to her. It runs:

A declaratory sentence of our holy Lord Pope Pius V, against Elizabeth, pretended queen of England, and all heretics adhering to her. By virtue of which sentence all her subjects are absolved from their oath of allegiance, and all other engagements whatsoever: and those who for the future shall obey her are excommunicated.

The bull declares that supreme authority over all nations is given by God to the Pope: that Elizabeth is guilty of harbouring Protestants and promoting the Protestant faith in her realm, of abolishing the sacrifice of the mass and other Roman Catholic rites, of claiming authority and jurisdiction over the Church of England, and refusing to admit to her kingdom the papal ambassador. The bull pronounced her, and her subjects who adhered to her, accursed, and deprived her of her right to the kingdom. Her subjects were absolved from all obligation of allegiance and commanded not to obey her orders.

It was a deliberate attempt, as Pius himself frequently acknowledged, to create a state of civil war in this country, and to overthrow the legitimate sovereign and government. It was an incitement to murder and rebellion. As Bishop Jewel wrote at the time, 'Peter and Paul taught obedience and respect to all lawful rulers, even non-Christian rulers, but the Pope who claims to sit in their chair declares the opposite. That can only be because he considers his authority above that of Scripture'. Such power is arbitrary and lawless.

Does the Pope today regard this sentence of his predecessor, Pius V, as morally wrong? We need to know, because so far the papacy has given no indication that it wishes to dissociate itself from the moral stance of that bull.

In addition to the bull itself there was the sequel to it, which is not without its echoes in the present time. On 12 December 1580 certain 'gentlemen of England' approached the papal nuncio in Madrid to inform him that they had entered into a pact to assassinate Elizabeth, and wished for an assurance that, if they were successful in the attempt, which might cost them their lives, they would not incur sin. The following is the answer, written by the Cardinal Secretary of State, to the papal nuncio:

Since that guilty woman of England rules over two such noble kingdoms of Christendom and is the cause of so much injury to the Catholic faith, and loss of so many million souls, there is no doubt that whosoever sends her out of the world with the pious intention of doing God service, not only does not sin but gains merit, especially having regard to the sentence pronounced against her by Pius V of holy memory. And so if those English gentlemen decide actually to take in hand so glorious a work, your Lordship can assure them that they do not commit any sin. We trust also in God that they will escape danger.

We need to know where the papacy today stands with regard to these matters, and the Pope surely owes us a statement before he visits this country. It would seem that a clear declaration by the Pope, that the judgment of his predecessor, Pius V, and the bull published by him, were wrong and wicked, would do more good and have greater relevance to the present than any number of general condemnations of violence, such as the Pope was so ready to utter during his visit to the Irish Republic.

The acts of the papacy in the past do have a relevance and bearing upon the contemporary situation. We should be foolish not to recognise it, and unwise to accept bland assurances that these things do not matter any more. Does it not matter any more that, when the news of the notable crime of the massacre of 10,000 Protestants, in Paris, on the eve of St Bartholomew's day in 1572, reached Rome, the Pope ordered a *Te Deum* to be sung, and commanded a procession to be held to thank God for the grace bestowed upon Christendom? Such crimes cannot be dismissed as irrelevant to the papacy today, because they were committed in the name and office of the papacy. Such crimes are not in the same category as the personal crimes, the notoriously immoral and scandalous lives, of many of the medieval Popes. It is true that these latter reflect adversely upon the office of religion these men held, but they are different in character from the terrible and heinous crimes we have referred to which were committed in the name of the church and the papal office itself.

It seems unlikely however that the Pope will declare himself on these questions, because the papacy cannot allow itself to be judged in faith and morals by anything outside itself, not even the Word of God. What the Pope teaches is considered true and right, not because it is found in Scripture, but because the Pope teaches it. The papacy is supreme over the Word of God. Thus the Church of Rome has got itself into an antinomian or lawless position, in which the will of the papacy is the sole arbiter of truth and righteousness, and consequently there is no power in earth or heaven which can reform or correct it. That is why the Reformers referred to 2 Thessalonians 2:4 as being the prophetic cameo of the papacy:

> Who opposeth and exalteth himself above all that is called God, or that is worshipped: so that he as God sitteth in the temple of God, shewing himself that he is God.

After this the bull *Apostolicae Curae* of 1896, declaring Anglican orders to be utterly null and void, and its sacraments to be no sacraments at all, seems of little or no importance. Nevertheless it must seem odd that the Pope can pay an ecumenical visit to Canterbury and yet say nothing about a matter like this either. Many Anglicans say they find it offensive and scandalous. I cannot myself share the view. It seems reasonable to recognise that a Protestant ministry is not the same in intention or execution as a Roman Catholic one. If the Pope were to say, as indeed he must, that his predecessor Pope Leo XIII was right in his judgment about Anglican orders, what would that matter? It was clearly not the intention of the Reformers to ordain sacrificing priests, but to abolish the mass in the English Church.

The constitutional dimension

There is another aspect of the papal visit to Britain and that is the political one. In what capacity or mode is the Pope supposed to be visiting this country? Cardinal Hume says that he is coming here on a purely pastoral visit, at the invitation of the Roman Catholic bishops. But it must be clear that the Royal Supremacy being what it is, and the claims of the papacy being what they are, not only should there be no official visit to Britian, but there should be no unofficial visit either.

The royal supremacy means that the Queen is supreme in all causes, ecclesiastical and spiritual as well as temporal, throughout her realm. There is no one in church or state superior to her. The Pope, by virtue of his claim to be the Vicar of Christ on earth, asserts that he is the supreme authority appointed by God over the whole universal church, and that includes the Church of England. Thus there is a fundamental conflict between the two claims. No visit by a Pope to this country should take place unless that conflict is resolved, for as things are the Pope must regard the British sovereign as a usurper (as Pius V pronounced in his bull of excommunication), and the crown must regard the Pope as an imposter. Do we now consider that the royal supremacy is no longer of any importance? We seem to behave as if we do in allowing the Pope who denies the authority of the Queen in her own realm to come here. Yet the Church of Rome does not itself seem in any hurry to waive the claims of the papacy or to state that they do not matter. In an interview on BBC television which I shared with Cardinal Hume I twice asked him if the Church of Rome still took seriously the claim of the Pope to be the Vicar of Christ, the Father of Princes, and Ruler of the world. He declined to answer. But there was a splendid opportunity for him to have assured the British people that the papacy no longer makes such a claim, that it is the relic of a bygone, feudal age.

As Mr Enoch Powell has pointed out, it was a prevarication to pretend that by describing the visit as a pastoral one it could be divested of its public character and political implications. I wonder if Cardinal Hume expected to be taken seriously when he said, in justification of what he had done in extending such an invitation, that many heads of state come here privately to do their Christmas shopping. The 'purely pastoral visit' was no more than a device for smuggling the Pope into the country, but from the beginning it was clearly intended that the visit should have a public character, and as wide a public character as it was possible to give it.

The invitation, when it was announced publicly by Cardinal Hume, on August 31, 1980, appeared to be an initiative which the Roman Catholic hierarchy itself had taken. The Government seemed in no way involved. Yet an invitation of that nature could not have been made without the approval of the Government first being given. As Mr Powell again pointed out, it was a ministerial decision which made the invitation possible; without such a favourable decision it is unthinkable that the Pope would have accepted or that the invitation would have been publicly announced.

Such a decision cannot be taken without reflecting adversely upon the Crown, for it undervalues and thereby downgrades the royal supremacy, which is the cornerstone of the British constitution. The position of the sovereign in the national Church buttresses the position of the sovereign in the nation. If the true constitutional position of the crown can be conveniently ignored and forgotten on this occasion, then it can be disregarded in other ways. It is a short step from undervaluing an institution to dispensing with it. The implications of this decision have yet to reveal themselves fully, but for those who might wish to see the royal supremacy replaced with papal primacy in the Church of England this is a necessary and logical step. The question is: Do we the British people wish to see that happen? If we do not then we should take the trouble to see that the integrity of our constitution is preserved and the sovereign is not placed in a position where it appears that the royal supremacy is no longer of any consequence, as would be the case if the Queen were to meet the Pope while he is in the country.

The ecumenical dimension

At the time the papal visit was announced, it was stated by Cardinal Hume and welcomed by the Archbishop of Canterbury, that the visit would have an ecumenical dimension. Soon afterwards Dr Runcie expressed the hope that the Pope would visit Canterbury Cathedral, though he did not say for what purpose. *The Times'* diarist speculated on December 24, 1980, that it might be for the purpose of saying a Roman Catholic mass. Three Church of England societies responded to this with a letter in the same newspaper pointing out that the saying of a Roman Catholic mass in Canterbury Cathedral, or indeed in any other Anglican place of worship, would constitute an ecclesiastical offence. In the February meeting of the General Synod, the Archbishop made it clear that there would be no papal mass at Canterbury. Instead, there would be an ecumenical service in which he and the Pope would take part. Had plans been made to hold a papal mass in Canterbury Cathedral? We cannot be sure, but it seems likely.

In many respects the ecumenical aspect of the Pope's visit is the most important. It would appear that it is intended to have a decisive significance for relations between the Church of England and the Church of Rome. What happens between these two churches will have repercussions for the whole religious situation in Britain. This centres principally on the three 'Agreed Statements' of the Anglican/Roman Catholic International Commission. The Archbishop of Canterbury is of the opinion that theological agreement has been reached by the commission and that this is now a firm foundation on which to build unity between the two churches. He considers that the remaining differences are cultural and moral rather than doctrinal, as he stated in an interview with the Roman Catholic Newspaper, *The Universe* in September 1981.

Reports from Rome suggest that the Pope also views favourably the work of the commission, and of course there is really no reason why he should not, for as we have seen the concessions are in favour of Roman Catholic doctrine. He is likely to give the 'Agreed Statements' his personal approval sometime immediately before he visits Britain. And as the Religious Affairs Correspondent of *The Times* has put it, 'A favourable final report from the theologians . . . published with papal approval in the months just before the Pope's visit, could add an excitement to the occasion which few could have foreseen when the original invitation was accepted'.

Few, no doubt, but nevertheless some, who understood that this would be the nature of the 'ecumenical dimension', and who, even before it was publicly announced, reckoned on a papal visit to this country effecting some significant development in the relations between the two churches. *The Times'* article goes on to speculate, 'If the ARCIC theologians from both sides are saying that no doctrinal barriers remain to prevent this extraordinary historic rapprochement, and that such disagreements as remain are entirely legitimate differences in understanding, containable within one united communion, then the Pope's presence in England will be seen by many Anglicans as an event in the internal life of the Church of England. To them he (the Pope) will be not just "the Roman Catholic Pope" but "our Pope".'

Of course, the Archbishop of Canterbury, for his part, has made no secret of his strong desire to see such a rapprochement come about. He has stated that he is deeply committed to reunion with Rome for both personal and theological reasons. In the same address in Westminster Abbey in 1981, in which he said this, he also declared that the time had come to grasp the nettle of the remaining differences between the Church of England and the Church of Rome. At the Anglican Consultative Council in Durham in October 1981 he expressed the wish that the Anglican Communion might eventually lose its identity in the one universal church, and in the interview with *The Universe*, to which we have referred, he hoped that he would himself be able to celebrate mass and receive communion in a Roman Catholic Church. These remarks, bearing as they do on one theme, are a necessary preparation for the papal visit in 1982 and are significant pointers to the ecumenical significance that will be attached to it, for then the Pope and the Archbishop will take, as Dr Runcie has put it, 'a step towards unity'.

The papal visit is the hinge upon which these hopes and expectations turn. The difficulty to date with the ecumenical movement is that it does not seem to have been going anywhere. It has been a talking shop, and the talking has gone on so long that people have become sceptical about anything ever happening. In order to gain credibility there has to be movement. But this cannot be brought about simply by theological discussions and doctrinal statements. There has to be a psychologically propitious moment when something is actually done, some occasion which will supply the required momentum. The papal visit is just such an occasion; it is an opportunity which, for those who want to see reunion with Rome, cannot be missed, for it may never return.

On the basis of the 'Agreed Statements' some commitment could be made during the visit, which might be regarded as initiating a new era in ecumenical relationships; which would signify a definite breach with the Reformation; and which would introduce a new phase in which the Church of England would become ever more closely linked with the Church of Rome. Such a change of direction requires a watershed and the papal visit provides it. In the euphoria and excitement generated by the visit criticism is less likely to be heard and considered.

It is just possible however that this could be a miscalculation of the mood in the churches. There are some signs of disquiet and concern about the way things have been moving, even amongst those sections of the church which appear to be unaligned or even positively ecumenical. The roots of the Protestant tradition go deep and spread even under those areas where they are not suspected to exist. What other explanation can be given to this editorial which appeared in the *Church Times* in 1981:

> Dr Runcie needs no telling that, even if he were minded to abandon the Free Churches in favour of Rome, he would have no authority to do so. The heritage of the Reformation, and of later Evangelical movements . . . within Anglicanism, is not going to be packed up and given away to be taken back to the Vatican along with the other souvenirs. No archbishop and no Pope-pilgrim in Canterbury, however able or popular, should be seen as capable of concluding a binding agreement.

That is a shot across the bows. There could be broadsides to come.

The policy of the present Pope

The Pope people see on their television sets is, as far as we can judge, an affable man with an attractive personality. A smile and a wave of the hand are his characteristic gestures. He has a manner which is ideally suited to the media. He stands in stark contrast to previous Popes who were remote and stern figures, except of course for his immediate predecessor, John Paul I, and John XXIII.

But there is another side to the character of the present Pope which may not be known to many people if they do not follow the affairs of the Roman Catholic Church. He is a conservative in doctrine and morals. This is not surprising in view of his Polish background. Poland is more traditionally Roman Catholic than Ireland. Ninety per cent of the population belong to the Church of Rome. So far the Pope has shown himself determined to maintain the traditional teaching of the Church and not give way to pressure for change from progressive clergy and laity.

This is seen in his unyielding attitude towards contraception, divorce, priestly celibacy, and the ordination of women. Some have tried to challenge him publicly, like the nun Sister Teresa Kane in America, who subjected him to an harangue on the ordination of women. But the Pope remains unmoved and pursues the path he has set himself of bringing the Roman Catholic Church back into line after many of the excesses that followed the Second Vatican Council.

His traditional, conservative approach has shown itself in his dealings with Hans Küng, the dissident priest and intellectual, who was deprived of his authority to teach as a Roman Catholic theologian, though the Church could do nothing to deprive him of his post which he holds in the University of Tübingen. Küng is of the opinion that the Church, while championing human rights in the world, denies them to its own people. The Pope's intransigence on the celibacy of priests he regards as violating the human right to marry.

The conservative character of the Pope was specially

marked in his visit to Ireland. There he made strong appeals to a population which, especially among the young people, is drifting away from the Roman Catholic faith under the changes affecting Irish society. 'The Ireland John Paul II sought to leave behind him was uncompromisingly Roman Catholic. No concessions were made to the modern age, nor was there any practical quarter for rival denominations. "Let no one ever doubt", he told a Dublin gathering of Irish Protestant leaders, "the commitment of the Catholic Church and of the Apostolic See of Rome to the pursuit of the unity of Christians" . . . Yet there was still room for doubt—unless unity was taken as meaning the universal acknowledgment that Rome was right'. John Whale continues this account of the Pope's visit:

> Catholic bishops and priests in Ireland refused to treat Protestant Christianity as being of equal worth with Catholic. The children of inter-Church marriages were in practice still required to be brought up as Catholics . . . No countenance was given to the notion that Catholic children might sometimes, as an experiment in neighbourliness, be educated with Protestant children . . . the Catholic position on that was not open to negotiation.
>
> Time could not be found for the Pope to visit an ecumenical vigil . . . and his meeting with Protestant leaders, brief and late at night, could not have occupied a lower place on his schedule . . .[1]

Protestants would be wise to be objective and discerning in their assessment of the Pope, and not capitulate to the ready smile and charm of the man. There are nuances in the speeches which need to be recognised. There is a strong and determined will behind the pleasing appearance committed to restoring the primacy and claims of the papacy. The year 2000 has a particular fascination for him. He sees in that the culmination of his vision of a reunited Christendom, reunited in the Roman Catholic Church and the Pope.

There are indications that the conservative element in the Church of Rome is now gaining the ascendency. Eighteen years work has just been completed on the revision of Canon Law. Several top churchmen are anxious about its publication as they consider it reflects a pre-Vatican II attitude to non-Roman Catholic Christians, whom it sees as individuals separated by error from the 'one true Church'.

More and more it appears that what Rome means by ecumenism is a return to the Roman Catholic Church and the acceptance of its teachings. Every indication given by Protestants of a willingness to hold their own faith cheap encourages the Church of Rome to believe that unity is yet possible on her terms.

10: The way forward

I have tried to show in this book that the differences between Roman Catholicism and Protestantism are not accidental or superficial. They arise from two diametrically opposed systems of religious doctrine which are mutually exclusive of each other. They are like oil and water: they will not mix. Attempts to reconcile them from the time of the Reformation to the present day have tended to take one or other of two courses—either to play down the differences and pretend that they are not real, or, if the real differences are recognised, to try to reconcile them in some ambiguous formula. But we are not free to deal with the truth in this way, for it is by and from the truth of God's Word that the Church must live, and discharge its responsibility to preach the Gospel to every creature.

Clarity about the nature of the Gospel and the way of salvation is, therefore, a duty and a matter of priority, and cannot be waived in the interest of any other thing 'Ye shall know the truth, and the truth shall make you free'. If we surrender the truth, which God has revealed in the Scriptures, for any purpose whatsoever, we lose our own freedom and the potential freedom of those to whom we must preach the message of deliverance through Christ crucified and risen.

Gospel ministry or priestly power

Here we are again compelled to face the crux of the difference between Roman Catholicism and Protestantism. What Protestantism regards as a *finished* work, the redemption of mankind by the once for all death of Christ upon the cross, now to be *proclaimed* (the New Testament word is *kerygma*, a heraldic announcement), the Roman Catholic Church sees as a possession to be *appropriated* by a hierarchical priesthood, and *dispensed* only through such priestly mediation. The principle at stake is an important, indeed, vital one, and that is free grace. What Protestantism holds was done freely for man by God, in the death of his Son, and is freely available to all in the word and promise of the Gospel, Rome claims is the special prerogative and province of the priest to mediate, and that apart from such credentials of priestly authority and office as she determines there are no valid sacraments and no assurance of grace. That is not merely to tie grace to an order of men, but also to pervert it. By making grace into a kind of commodity which can be dispensed by the priestly power of the church they have changed its character, so that it is no longer grace, for certainly it is no longer free. We find no such limits and curbs set upon the operation of grace in the New Testament, where it is associated not with priests but with heralds or preachers of the Good News.

Let us imagine that some government was able to persuade the people over whom it ruled that, in order to breathe, they must be equipped with a respirator which was available only from the government itself. A tank of air would be supplied with the respirator, which would need to be replenished regularly, but this operation could only be performed by authorised agents of the government. How astonished the first man would be who dared to throw off his respirator and discover that he could breathe without it; that God's air is free! That, in principle, is the difference between Roman Catholicism and Protestantism. The whole difference turns upon this question of priesthood. The Roman Catholic Church, by erecting the principle of priesthood and making it essential to its ministry, thereby makes the laity wholly dependent upon the priesthood for spiritual life and grace. Protestantism knows no such priesthood because it is alien to the spirit and the letter of the New Testament. There is no essential difference between the minister and the people, only a difference of function. There is nothing in principle that the minister does which the people cannot do. But, that things may be done decently and in order, it is fit and proper that no man should take

124

to himself the office of ministering in the congregation. He must first be properly called and publicly set apart by the church for the work of the ministry. These then are the two poles around which the different concepts of ministry cluster—the Roman Catholic notion of the priest, which seeks its authority and justification in tradition, and the Protestant understanding of the minister, which claims its authenticity from the nature of the Gospel and from Scripture.

The priestly principle represents the monopolisation of God and of God's grace. It is the same in essence as the desire of Simon Magus (Acts 8:18), to gain possession of the Spirit of God in order that he could then control and dispense that gift. What was wrong with him was not just his offer of money, but that he had a pagan conception of ministry as priestly power over God. Wherever that spirit manifests itself in religion, or in the church, today it owes its origin to paganism not to Christianity, to the spirit of antichrist not to the Spirit of Christ. 'Roman Catholicism is a terrible thing', said Karl Barth, 'because it means the imprisonment of God Himself. It claims to be the possessor of the Holy Spirit and revelation and Jesus Christ Himself. Can anything be more terrible than the identification of God and man?'[1]

What we see taking place today in the ecumenical movement is a general drift towards the priestly conception of ministry. In the proposals for reunion with Rome Protestants are being asked to surrender the Gospel view of ministry and endorse the priestly understanding. In other schemes of reunion, too, the same movement in the direction of sacerdotalism can be seen, for at some stage there is insistence upon the *necessity* of invariable episcopal ordination. This is a warning sign. It reveals that the attraction is towards the pole that has its logical centre in the Roman Catholic view of priesthood, and ultimately the papacy. Those who seek to reconstruct the ministry of a united church along these lines, who insist upon this particular understanding of priestly ordination by a bishop and its necessity in any reunited church, should beware of what they are laying up for the future. They are setting in motion

125

a movement towards exclusivism of priestly orders and the spiritual totalitarianism which has always been associated with it.

There is, as Professor Gordon Rupp has said, a worse bondage than subjection to the state, and that is when the church becomes the tool of its own perverted powers. The modern democratic state affords some protection to Roman Catholics against their own church. The Pope was only able to deprive Hans Küng of his teaching office as a Roman Catholic theologian. He was not able to remove him from his post as a Professor at the University of Tübingen. But what if that power were made stronger in a universal church so as to be uncontested? Might not the dream of ecumenism then become a nightmare? What right have we to say it cannot happen if we are working, wittingly or unwittingly, to bring about its realisation? Only the spirit of Protestantism can preserve us from such a fate. If the principles and doctrines of Protestantism decay through neglect, or are discarded by those who should maintain them, then the danger of which we have spoken becomes a distinct possibility.

The maintenance of the Protestant conception of a Gospel ministry over against that of the priestly power of the Church of Rome is the only guarantee of the liberty of the church. 'If I build again the things which I destroyed, I make myself a transgressor.' If we willingly concur, or even unresistingly comply in the process of restoring sacerdotalism, then we are guilty of forging the links in the chain which will eventually bind us and future generations.

Can there, then, never be reunion between Roman Catholicism and Protestantism? We can conceive of terms under which that would be possible. It would be possible if one side or the other gave up the principles which are at the heart of its system, and were converted to the opposite principles; if, for example, the Pope were to give up his claim to be the Vicar of Christ and to supreme and universal jurisdiction over the church; if the Roman Catholic bishops were to renounce their claim to be high priests and to ordain sacerdotal priests, and become simply preachers of the

126

Word and ministers of the sacraments. If that were to happen then reunion would be possible. But if the reaction is to say that this is unthinkable, that Rome would never renounce any of these claims, then it should be equally unthinkable that Protestantism should surrender its liberty in the Gospel and be drawn into acceptance of, and subservience to, a priestly ministry and papal authority. However it may be presented, whether in terms of pre- or post-Vatican II, the price of reunion with Rome remains the same. The requirement is to return to Mother Church. If Rome relaxes that demand she ceases to be Rome.

Displaying the Truth

Faced with this impasse the only response open to Protestantism, which does not compromise its integrity, is to commend to Roman Catholics the liberty that we enjoy in the Gospel. Just at a time when the Roman Catholic Church is showing greater openness we should be affirming the positive message of Protestantism and clarifying our faith both for ourselves and them, rather than obscuring it in a fog of ecumenical diplomacy and compromise. We should take a leaf out of the notebook of John XXIII, who said that the purpose of Vatican II was to clarify the faith of Roman Catholicism so as to reveal its true nature and allow it to make its own intrinsic appeal to the 'separated brethren'. We have looked at the result and we still do not care for what we see. But that is because we believe that Protestantism provides us with something higher, better, purer, stronger, freer. We must therefore present our faith in the belief that when we do so it will make its own intrinsic appeal to Roman Catholics.

Justification by free grace and the priesthood of all believers are glorious and liberating doctrines of the Gospel. If we ourselves have experienced their power, been apprehended by their truth, and cheered by their light, then we should be able to commend them to others in their biblical simplicity and authority, rather than be partners in some scheme by which their power will be sapped, their truth obscured and their light hidden. God has not given us the glorious Gospel of free grace that it might be hidden. Our business is to display it prominently in all its fulness and radiance. It is the business of the churches to do this. And if they do not preach the 'pure Word' and seek to preserve it in its liberty and glory in this land, then God will judge them by removing them, for that is their sole purpose.

There are some indications that the Church of Rome is on the defensive in this respect, and would be even more so if the Protestant churches were to take the initiative in presenting the Gospel. She is aware that the doctrine of the priesthood of all believers has a powerful appeal. She therefore speaks of the 'common priesthood' of the laity. This does not mean that she has done away with the hierarchical priesthood. Far from it. She emphasises it and its essential difference from the so-called common priesthood of the people. But by such language she indicates that she is conscious of the potency of the biblical doctrine. That should encourage us to go on and maintain our position, to commend it positively and to be aware of its strength. In terms of spiritual warfare Protestantism has nothing to fear from Roman Catholicism, it merely requires deployment by those who know its worth and have experienced its truth.

These then are the principles that should guide us in all our dealings with the Church of Rome and with individual Roman Catholics. The greater freedom of contact that now exists between Roman Catholics and Protestants is something which we must welcome. Whether this is in fact due to the ecumenical movement itself, or whether other factors are equally involved is arguable. It is quite possible that changes generally in society—the breaking down of social and class divisions, the growth of communications, the greater mobility of people—have all had something to do with the revolution in social manners and relations since the Second World War, and the churches themselves have not been exempted from these influences. It would appear that there would have been a greater openness anyway in society, and the Church of Rome could not forever maintain a fence around its people. Perhaps the greatest contributory factor of all in closer contact between members of all churches has been the growing secularism of society, which has both isolated them and also thrown them together. We accept the situation as a datum. It is one, however, which lends itself naturally to the commendation of our faith to Roman Catholics.

In order to do this we must understand the doctrines of Protestantism and above all be guided by principle not pragmatism. The primacy of the truth of the Gospel must at all times determine our response to Roman Catholicism. The weakness of Protestantism in the ecumenical debate, and the continual sacrifice of its positions before the steady advance of Rome, have been due to an undoctrinal and haphazard approach. When the systematic and positive character of Protestant doctrine is understood, so as to become once again a coherent whole in the life and experience of the Protestant churches, then we shall be able to establish our true position *vis à vis* Roman Catholicism and effectively commend our faith.

Practical consequences

In practice this means that we must do nothing to compromise the Gospel. Meeting, praying and studying the Bible informally with Roman Catholics do not compromise the Gospel. Joint services of worship in each others churches, or allowing Roman Catholic services, such as the mass, to be held in Protestant places of worship do, because they suggest that there is fundamentally no difference in these matters between the Church of Rome and Protestantism. Doctrinal discussions with Roman Catholic clergy or lay people on an informal level do not compromise the Gospel. It might surprise many to know that public discussions of this nature took place frequently from Catholic Emancipation in 1829 until well into the 1840s when the Roman Catholic hierarchy put a stop to it. Protestantism has nothing to fear from open, public discussion of differences; indeed it has everything to gain. What is a threat to Protestantism are theological commissions set up for the purpose of arriving at agreement. Such commissions are appointed by the ruling bodies of the different churches, whose sympathies, on the Protestant side, often lie in a Romeward direction. The appointees are men who fit in with the trends of the establishment, otherwise they would not be where they are. The ingredients put into the mix determine what the result will be. Wherever such tendencies prevail Protestantism must suffer because its doctrines and principles are considered expendable.

The way forward for Protestantism is to have more open discussion and public debate of the issues, and to be less involved in schemes and commissions which inhibit the spirit of free enquiry and stifle the expression of real and legitimate doctrinal differences—differences which cannot be successfully contained in some contrived and fragile formula.

Joint evangelism is another area where Protestants ought not to become involved with the Church of Rome because we are not agreed about the Gospel. The Roman Catholic Church, if it is true to its principles, must preach a message of man's co-operation with God in salvation. Salvation in the Church of Rome is by faith *and* works. This is not 'Good News'. It is bad news to be told that God gives me a start, but after that it depends on me. I know I cannot do it, and shall fail. Even with the help of God I shall fail. It must be done *for* me; more than that, it must be completed for me before I come to it. I must hear the words 'it is finished' pronounced upon my redemption before I can really believe that I am saved or can be saved. The Gospel does that. It declares a redemption complete, entire and finished even before I had any disposition to receive it. 'While we were yet sinners, Christ died for us', and that redemption 'justifies the ungodly' (Romans 4:5), not the godly. That alone is good news for the sinner.

The Church of Rome has no such message. It cannot declare that message without annihilating itself and all its machinery of priestly mediation. 'Half a loaf is better than no loaf', but half a Gospel is not better than no Gospel, because it predisposes men against the true Gospel. It is in the same category as a half-truth which deceives. The mes-

sage of the Church of Rome is self-salvation with a measure
of help from God. But that makes God our helper, co-
operating with man, and not the sovereign Redeemer and
Saviour. This is the reason why Mary figures so prominently in Roman Catholicism. She is styled co-redemptrix,
co-operating with God in the redemption of the world.
Thus she becomes the type above all of the Roman Catholic
co-operating with God in his salvation.

There can be no shared or joint evangelism with the
Church of Rome for she preaches another gospel: a gospel
which has no power to set men free but, on the contrary,
enmeshes the individual into a legalistic system and subjection to the priest.

Value of the Protestant Confessions

If there is to be a renewal and advance of Protestantism in
the nation then a necessary condition of it must be the
return of the Reformation Confessions of Faith to their
rightful places in the Churches. We do not seek to per-
petuate such things for their own sake, as an end in themselves, but because we regard the doctrines they enshrine
as formulating the essence of the true Gospel, which must
be preached by the churches if the nation is to be evange-
lised. Our neglect of them has attended our decline, their
reinstatement will facilitate a return to true religion. As we
have moved away from them so we have moved away from
the Gospel, either to the left into mere moralism and humanism, or to the right into sacerdotalism.

We do not regard the Confessions as on a level with
Scripture, for that would be to repeat the Roman Catholic
error regarding tradition. But while they are subordinate to
Scripture and always subject to judgment and revision under Scripture, we see them as encapsulating the essential
biblical doctrines regarding man, sin and salvation. Where
we cannot improve upon them we have a duty to adhere to
them, and so far attempts to improve upon them have taken
us into paths leading to spiritual failure and weakness.

The Confessions should be regarded as maps or guides
which lead us on the journey of faith. They are valuable in

that they indicate the route we must take to true faith, but they are not a substitute for faith or for real existential encounter with the living Word of God. Tyndale wrote many introductions to the books of the Bible, setting out the principal teachings of those books about grace and faith, about sin and salvation. Those doctrinal treatises he termed 'Pathways into Scripture'. That was a particularly happy expression. That is what the doctrinal Confessions and formularies of Protestantism are. They are no more than helps to find the true and living way in Scripture, which is Christ himself set forth as our Saviour in the Gospel of redemption and free grace.

If we neglect our map we lose our way, and if we neglect doctrine we shall lose the way of salvation. 'Take heed unto thyself, and unto doctrine; continue in them for in doing this thou shalt both save thyself, and them that hear thee' (1 Timothy 4:16). It is the special responsibility of those who are teachers and guides to be sure they know the way in order that they may safely lead others and not be 'blind leaders of the blind'. That is why this discussion of Roman Catholicism and Protestantism has been doctrinal. It could not be any other, without neglecting the one thing essential to it.

Living faith

When we speak of the reinstatement of the Reformation Confessions as the only way forward for Protestantism we mean not merely the recovery of the letter but the spirit. We are concerned with recapturing in our generation the vital religion and living faith which they represent. Language, however beautiful and however true, cannot of itself sustain religion. But language is a vehicle of spirit. It brings with it the possibility of regeneration. We must at least begin here if we are to experience again the virtue, the power, the truth and the force of such religion. These are the things which belong to our peace and they have for so long been hidden from our eyes.

The advice given to the young John Wesley when he complained of lack of saving faith was, preach faith until you have it. He did and he found it. Similar advice was given to John Bradford, the English Reformer. If the churches are ready once again to declare the doctrines of free grace then they will experience the reality, the power and the truth of these things. As they go their way (the way in which God has directed they should go in his Word), they shall be made whole. In this time of spiritual poverty and weakness in the churches that is the only way to renewal. The path of ecumenical politics and compromise with Rome is the path to further spiritual decline and bankruptcy. We must return to the answer we already possess, before it is too late.

'What a fool I am', said Christian in the dungeon of Doubting Castle, 'to lie here all this time when I may as well walk at liberty. I have a key in my possession called Promise which will open every lock in Doubting Castle'. Protestantism has been in a similar situation. The spiritual weakness and depression from which it suffers, the prison of impotency in which it has been confined, are things from which it can be liberated now. It has the key to the problem in its own possession, at its very heart, in the Reformation Confessions of Faith which it must again appropriate experimentally. The note of certainty and authority which Protestantism lacks today can be recovered, when there is a return to the religious faith and experience of the Reformers, which is the true and authentic religion of the Bible.

If the Protestant churches will concentrate their mind and energies upon this task the result will be seen in renewed authority and power by which to bring the Word of God to our generation.

Appendix: A summary of differences between Roman Catholicism and Protestantism

Justification by faith alone

When people assert that there are now no real differences between the Church of Rome and the Protestant churches it is difficult to know what they mean, because the central difference which led to the Reformation itself, justification by faith, remains unresolved and, to my mind, never can be resolved except by one side or the other giving up its position. Perhaps there are those Protestants who are prepared to do this, but that must surely be because they do not understand the worth of what they are so ready to surrender. If on the other hand we understand our heritage rightly then we are not free to give it up, because we cannot do as we like with the truth.

'How can I be right with God?' is the first and most important question in religion, and the doctrine of justification by faith alone is the answer to it. If you have ever asked that question yourself then you will realize how vital the right answer is. The wrong answer is disastrous. We dare not pretend that the difference is not important, or assume that we have licence to change its meaning, however slightly, in order to come to some arrangement with the Church of Rome.

We have a very clear statement of the Protestant doctrine in Article XI of the Church of England, which follows closely the Augsburg Confession:

> We are accounted righteous before God only for the merits of our Lord and Saviour Jesus Christ, by faith, and not for our own merits or deservings . . .

First, we must notice the word 'accounted'. This means that God counts or reckons us as righteous even though we are not righteous in ourselves, even though we are full of sin, and have never done anything good to deserve such reckoning. This righteousness which God imputes to us, Paul makes clear in Romans, is not our own at all, it is the free gift of God to sinners, to those who are unrighteous and undeserving. The whole point of Paul's argument is that God justifies not the good but the bad, not the righteous but the unrighteous, not the godly but the ungodly. If God merely justified the godly there would be nothing new or surprising in that. It would not have been a message which Paul could call a Gospel. But here he is declaring something that is simply astonishing both to himself and others, that God accepts sinful men as righteous, just as they are, without them becoming righteous in themselves first. That is a Gospel for those who know and feel themselves to be sinners and incapable of doing the least of God's commandments as it should be done.

Faith lays hold on this amazing declaration of God in the Gospel and says, I believe that it is true and accept it, because God says it, even though I find it astonishing. Such faith is not the mere assent of the mind to certain propositions, it is trust in God, trust in the promise that He has made in the Gospel. Faith of this kind contributes nothing to our salvation, it only enables us to accept the precious gift of justification. The ground on which God accepts us is not found in ourselves; it is in the perfect righteousness of the Lord Jesus Christ. As the Article puts it '. . . *only* for the merit of Our Lord and Saviour Jesus Christ'.

So justification owes nothing to us at all. It comes to us as a free gift, perfect and complete. It is counted to us at the beginning of our Christian lives, when we first believe in Christ, before we have done anything or can do anything to serve or please God, and remains perfect and complete throughout our entire lives and we can do nothing to improve or increase it. We can grow in holiness, in consecration to God, but we cannot improve or add to our justification for it is not strictly ours at all, it is the righteousness of Christ.

Faith will, of course, bring a new relationship with God,

135.

a new desire to please him and keep his commandments, for the Holy Spirit who is given to believers will move us to love and serve God. But none of this will be part of our justification. That depends from the beginning to the end of our lives upon Christ. God accepts us for no other cause, but only for the merit of our Lord and Saviour Jesus Christ.

The Roman Catholic Church does not teach this. It disputes the word 'accounted', and argues that we are not *accounted* or *reckoned* righteous by faith in Christ, but that we are *made* righteous in ourselves, and that this *inherent* righteousness is the ground of our justification. This raises the question of how we are made righteous, and their answer is, by receiving grace and strength through the sacraments so that we can do good works. At baptism they say the slate is wiped clean, as it were, and grace is then given to lead a Christian life. If mortal sins are committed then the individual loses his justification, but he can be restored by the sacrament of penance. But clearly such justification is something at which the individual has to work and it depends upon his effort, his obedience, his goodness. This is a legalistic doctrine and more akin to the state Paul found himslf in under the Jewish religion, rather than the freedom he came to know under the Gospel. It is certainly something totally different from the Biblical doctrine found in the Protestant faith. It is what Paul calls in Galatians 1 'another Gospel'. It turns our gaze from Christ, our righteousness, to ourselves, to our good works and deservings. It militates against the tenor of the of the true Gospel, as preached by Paul, and replaces the spirit of love with the spirit of fear.

We return to the first and fundamental question of religion: 'How can I be right with God?' Are we justified by our own righteousness or the righteousness of Christ? The answer the Bible and Protestantism give is unequivocal: We are accounted righteous before God only for the merit of our Lord and Saviour Jesus Christ, by faith, and not for our own merits or deservings.

When I say the answer Protestantism gives, I mean of course the classical Protestantism of the Confessions. Popular Protestantism today has largely forgotten about these things and has become a stranger in its own home, alienated from its own heritage. Nowadays many theological students betray almost entire ignorance of the meaning of the doctrine of justification by faith. But this fact must be evident in our churches where the subject is rarely mentioned from the pulpit. Thirty years ago I never heard it preached and only discovered it myself by reading the Reformers. The result of this is that popular Protestantism has repeated the mistakes of Roman Catholicism. In fact, it preaches a message not dissimilar. Put very simply it is this: Believe in Jesus and he will help you to be good. This in essence is no different from believing that the sacraments give you grace to live a Christian life. In both cases man's justification before God resides in himself, in the change that grace is able to work within. And in both cases the Lord Jesus Christ is only the means to an end, man's own righteousness.

It is not surprising that many Protestants today should find their own position and that of the Roman Church almost indistinguishable. But that is not because the Gospel has changed, or the truth of Protestant doctrine has changed, but because they have lost touch with it, or never knew it in the first place. But the seeds of recovery and renewal are within Protestantism itself, in its doctrines and Confessions. Within the Church of Rome there is only the formal and systematic denial of the truth.

Mary

The place accorded to Mary in the official teaching and popular devotion of the Roman Catholic Church must remain one of the major differences that separate it from Protestantism.

The references made to Mary in the Bible are few and simple. She is depicted as a devout, virtuous and believing woman on whom was conferred the special honour of becoming the mother of our Lord. But nowhere is there any suggestion that she should be worshipped, prayed to, or regarded as a mediator.

Gradually, over the centuries, the devotion paid to Mary, and the teaching of the Roman Catholic Church about her, have grown until now they obscure the person and office of Christ as Saviour. This is not surprising when people are taught to come to Christ through Mary, and that the surest way of prayers being answered is, that they should be addressed to Christ through Mary.

The Rosary, which is the most common prayer ritual of Roman Catholics, has ten prayers to Mary for each one devoted to God. More candles are lit before statues of Mary than before statues of Christ. This is the kind of prominence the cult of the Virgin Mary has assumed in the Roman Catholic Church, and we can see how it reverses the emphasis of Scripture, where everything points to Christ.

I suppose this is not surprising when we consider how the statue of the Virgin Mary with the Child in her arms is constantly before the bodily eye, and the mind's eye, of the Catholic worshipper. The impression created is that of the dominating, adult figure of Mary, with a subordinate place for Christ as the weak and helpless infant. Thus we see how images can be misleading, and can deny the truth of Scripture, (the prophets called them 'lying images'), so that we need to take seriously the warnings of the Bible against their subtle and insidious tendency to draw the mind away from God.

In the Middle Ages Christ was represented as the stern judge and Mary as the kind and compassionate mother, who would obtain mercy for the sinner from her Son. This emphasis is still present today even amongst the 'progressives' such as Schillebeeckx, the Dutch Roman Catholic theologian, who writes, 'The natural quality of love cannot be in the man Jesus—but it is in Mary'.[1]

The discovery by the Reformers that the Scriptures teach no such thing, but that Christ himself is our advocate and his blood the propitiation for our sins was something that revolutionised their thinking, and accounts for the prominence of biblical texts expressing this truth in our services, especially the comfortable words of the Holy Communion service of the Church of England.

In recent times the cult of the Virgin Mary has grown and assumed even greater proportions in the Roman Catholic Church. One of the important developments was the promulgation of the Dogma of the Immaculate Conception of the Virgin Mary in 1854, that is, that Mary was conceived and born without sin, and remained sinless throughout her life. Along with this it is claimed that Mary remained a virgin and had no other children, though the Scriptures speak of the brothers and sisters of Christ, and of Mary's marriage as a normal one after the birth of Jesus.

In 1950, Pope Pius XII declared the Dogma of the Bodily Assumption, that is, that Mary was taken bodily into heaven after her burial and crowned as the Queen of Heaven. There is nothing in the Bible to support such teaching. Without the least trace of embarrassment a Roman Catholic theologian has written of it, '. . . indeed, this most glorious Assumption of Mary is veiled in the mystery of silence: Scripture knows nothing of it'.[2] Yet it is declared by the Church of Rome that those who do not believe this dogma cannot be saved.

Many Protestants have the lingering feeling that the teaching of the Church of Rome on this subject cannot be as extreme as it appears. That the official teaching of the Church must be more moderate and, particularly, that Vatican II has done something to improve matters and remove excesses. Vatican II, in line with its declared aim of presenting with greater clarity the teaching of the Roman Catholic Church, warned against exaggeration on the one hand and narrow-mindedness on the other. But it failed to say what exactly these were, which hardly advances the cause of greater clarity. At the same time it reiterated all the traditional teaching regarding Mary. Such as, that:

> In an utterly singular way she cooperated by her obedience, faith, hope, and burning charity in the Saviour's work of restoring supernatural life to souls. For this reason she is a mother to us in the order of grace.

and

> This maternity will last without interruption until the eternal fulfilment of all the elect. For, taken up to heaven, she did not lay aside this saving role, but by her manifold acts of intercession continues to win for us gifts of eternal salvation . . .

Therefore the Blessed Virgin is invoked by the Church under the titles of Advocate, Auxiliatrix, Adjutrix and Mediatrix . . .

The decree hastens to assure us that this must not be understood as in any way detracting from the dignity and efficacy of Christ the one mediator. It supports this contention by saying that Mary shares in the mediation of Christ just as the priesthood of Christ is shared in various ways by the hierarchy, the bishops and priests. But this merely invokes one traditional and erroneous doctrine to support another. The more one investigates Catholic doctrine the more it becomes clear that the Church spins the web of its theology out of its own body.

The opinions of the various Marian schools are not condemned by Vatican II and the decree admonishes that the cult of the Virgin Mary be generously fostered.

What all this really means doctrinally is perhaps best brought out in the words of the present Pope John Paul II, who closes his book *Sign of Contradiction*, (which was a series of addresses given in Lent 1976 in the presence of Paul VI), with a powerful exposition of what the significance of mariolatry is for the Roman Catholic Church. After reminding Pope Paul VI that he had proclaimed Mary to be the Mother of the Church, he then goes on to draw out what that means. It means that God has put the Church under her care for all time. God 'demonstrated the greatest trust in mankind by giving mankind his Son . . . The human creature to whom he first entrusted him was Mary . . . and until the end of time she will remain the one to whom God entrusts the whole of his mystery of salvation . . .

'Within the dimensions of the universe the Son of God, the eternal Word, the Lord of the ages to come is her son and she is his mother. Therefore all that goes to make up what he bequeathed—the work of salvation, the Mystical Body of Christ, the People of God, the Church—is taken care of, and always will be taken care of, by her—with the same fidelity and strength that she showed in taking care of her son: from the stable in Bethlehem, to Calvary and to the upper room on the day of Pentecost when the Church was born, Mary is present in all the vicissitudes of the Church'.

This is an immense conception of the role of Mary, far greater than most Protestants understand, and it is something which inheres in the very stuff of Roman Catholicism. When the Church of Rome is wrong it is wrong on a grand scale, and the measure of this conception is the measure of its error. The image of the Madonna with the Child in her arms does not lie, according to Roman Catholic doctrine. It is a true reflection of the role of Mary. Seated upon the throne of heaven she embraces Christ and the Church. It is the reason why everything that happens in the Church is committed to the protection of Mary, 'the Immaculate Queen of the Church and the mother of unity', as was the Second Vatican Council itself in these very words by Pope John XXIII. It is the reason why the present Pope in his first public utterance, after the attempt upon his life in St Peter's Square, ascribed his deliverance to Mary and professed that he was 'totally hers'. This to most Protestants, even those who are sympathetic to the Pope, is unintelligible. It is however in Roman Catholic terms the natural and inescapable conclusion of Marian doctrine.

We have seen in recent years the revival of the cult of Mary in the Church of England. It has no foundation on which to rest in the doctrine of that church. But we have seen the Archbishop of Canterbury visit the 'Shrine of our Lady of Walsingham' and give an added impetus to this tendency by his presence there. All the traditional language is used about Mary leading us to Christ. But we must be clear about the direction of this tendency and realistic about what lies behind it. It stands biblical doctrine on its head, and, while professing innocence of idolatry, worships the creature more than the Creator.

The Papacy

The temptation for Protestants to look upon the Pope as simply a religious leader, rather on the lines of the Archbishop of Canterbury or the President of the Methodist

Conference, is one which has to be resisted, because the claims which the Roman Catholic Church makes for the papal office far exceed anything that is attributed to any other Christian leader, and place it in an entirely different category from the offices they hold.

The powers of the Pope are defined in the canon law of the Church of Rome as 'The supreme or full power of jurisdiction over the universal Church both in matters of faith and morals and in matters of discipline and government'.

Jurisdiction means the power to make laws. It is not leadership by moral influence or persuasion which the Pope claims, but the power to compel obedience and to bind the conscience of the individual. In other words, what the Pope teaches, the individual is bound to believe and obey.

This power, it is claimed, the Pope has over the universal Church. That means, in the first place, over the whole Roman Catholic Church, clergy and people, and all the organs of that church, no one and nothing is excepted. The College of Cardinals and even a Universal Council of the Church are subject to the supreme authority of the Pope. Although he was elected by the Cardinals he does not derive his authority from them, nor from the Church, but it is claimed that, as the successor of Peter, he receives it direct from Christ. The concept of the 'universal church' includes all baptized Christians, and the Pope claims jurisdiction over your conscience and mine even though we do not acknowledge the claim.

The Pope's authority is absolute and immediate in all matters of faith and morals, and in matters of discipline and government. That means that if the Pope teaches, as he does, that the Virgin Mary was taken up bodily into heaven, even though it is not in the Bible it must be believed. Or if the Pope teaches that his own teachings are infallible it must be believed. Similarly if the Pope teaches that artificial contraception is wrong within marriage, he must be obeyed. I have spoken to many Roman Catholics who say that they do not accept these things, particularly the moral directives of the Pope on birth control. But if that is their view they are in open conflict with the clear teaching of their Church. It means that they are bad Catholics, not that the Church of Rome has changed its position, or is likely to change its position.

This brings us to the word 'immediate', which is used to describe the Pope's authority, and means that the authority of the Pope over every person in the Church is direct. It touches each member without the need to go through any intermediate officer of the Church. So ultimately what matters in the Roman Church is what the Pope teaches, not what the parish priest or the bishop think. I mention this because sometimes it is thought that the individual can escape from the unpalatable things the Pope teaches by going to a priest who adopts a liberal interpretation and a lenient discipline. But strictly speaking there is no such refuge for the Roman Catholic conscience from clear papal teaching.

This concept of the immediate authority of the Pope is an important factor both in the interpretation of the decrees of Vatican II, and also in the implementation by progressive clergy of what they believed were the reforms that were to be introduced following the Council. Some of the bishops at Vatican II requested that attention should be given to modernising the diplomatic service of the Vatican. The legates or nuncios who perform the diplomatic services of the Vatican are the Pope's personal representatives to secular governments and local Catholic bishops throughout the world. As vicars or representatives of the Supreme Pontiff they carry his instructions and act with his full authority.

The Pope responded in a document entitled *Sollicitudo Omnium Ecclesiarum*, in which he stated, 'the proper and specific office of the Pontifical Representative is to render even closer and more operative the ties that bind the Apostolic See and the local churches'. The document also affirms that, 'the authority which the Pope exercises over the entire Church is one that is full, supreme, universal, ordinary and immediate'. These words are intended to impress upon all who read them that the Pope's authority reaches to every area of the Church's life in doctrine, liturgy and morals,

143

and can be challenged by none. Moreover, such authority derives from the normal function of the Pope's office and calls for total obedience. This statement coming only four years after the Second Vatican Council is a powerful confirmation of the traditional powers of the papacy.

The present Pope is determined to affirm and deploy the full authority of the papal office in order to restore uniformity after a period of licence and confusion following Vatican II. The papal legates will play an important part in this plan, since they carry with them the full and personal authority of the Pope himself.

It seems that the Pope's travels have opened his eyes to many things which are being done in the Church in the name of Vatican II, which are neither in accordance with its letter or its spirit. Some of these things have surprised and shocked him and he is convinced that the remedy must come from the centre, from the re-assertion of the prerogative of the papal office. This is possible because Vatican II has left the whole diplomatic machinery of the papacy intact. The doctrine of the papacy the Council had no power to change, but neither has there been any change in the system of papal representation through the function of the papal ambassadors. Thus the full and immediate authority of the Pope still has effective channels through which it can pass into nearly every country in the world.

In 1980 the Pope issued an Instruction *Inaestimabile Donum* in which he listed many of the things which he saw exceeded the limits of Vatican II, liturgically: ie. confusion of the roles of priests and laity; lay people and priests saying the eucharistic prayer together; lay people preaching; priests leaving off liturgical vestments; lack of reverence for the sacrament; unauthorised eucharistic prayers; liturgical texts being used for political ends; and much more besides. He called for obedience to the norms laid down, and for bishops to see that such instructions are carried out. The means are there for the Pope to see that such injunctions are not disregarded.

The confusion and the optimism of the immediate post-Vatican II period are subsiding. As Paul Johnson wrote recently, 'There are dramatic signs that Pope John-Paul II . . . intends to take drastic steps to restore discipline and uniformity among the world's 600 million Catholics and, in particular, to insist on a new standard of obedience and conformity among the bishops of the Church'. Johnson continues, 'This emerged strongly during the recent synod in Rome (1980), where progressive-minded prelates, who in recent years have had things very much their own way, were whipped into line by the pontiff on such issues as sexual morality, marriage law, and divorce. Many of them left Rome depressed and apprehensive. As one of them put it: "The era of reform which began with the election of Pope John XXIII is now definitely over" '.

Protestants should not mistake the voice of progressive theologians inside the Church of Rome for the voice of Rome itself. Pope John-Paul II has made it very clear, both by his words and actions, that he sees the role of the theologian as serving the *magisterium* (teaching office) of the Church which is centred in the papacy.[2]

One is sometimes tempted to wonder if Protestant Church leaders fully appreciate the formidable nature of the papacy, especially when they are given to rather loose talk about conceding to the Pope a 'primacy of honour' and recognising him as some kind of universal president of the churches. The proper nature and claims of the papacy cannot be reconciled with this sort of understanding. Its nature and function is, as we have seen, something quite different. Either the Pope is what he claims to be, the Vicar of Christ and the Vicegerent of God on earth, wielding full and immediate authority over the universal Church, or he is an imposter. There would seem to be no middle path. The decree of the First Vatican Council should leave us in no doubt: 'If anyone says . . . that (the Pope) received . . . only a primacy of honour and not a true and proper jurisdiction: let him be anathema'.

The Mass

Many Protestants today may consider the Mass to be just a more colourful and elaborate form of the Communion service that they themselves are familiar with. Such a view is however quite mistaken. The central concept and action of the mass is not communion but sacrifice. In the words of a Roman Catholic expositor, 'The mass . . . is a dramatic re-enactment in an unbloody manner of the sacrifice of Christ on Calvary'.

First, it is affirmed that the priest by virtue of his office has the power to change the bread and wine into the actual body and blood of Christ when he pronounces the words of consecration, 'This is my body', and 'This is my blood'. These words are interpreted as a command which makes the whole Christ present as a victim on the altar. The priest is then supposed to immolate, that is, to slay Christ and offer him up to God as a sacrifice for the expiation of sin, as really and effectually as Christ himself made his oblation of himself at Calvary. The term 'Host', applied to the consecrated wafer used in the mass, is a term of Latin derivation and means a sacrificial victim.

Thus the central action of the mass is the repetition of the sacrifice of Calvary. Christ, it is supposed, is crucified afresh to put away sin every time a mass is said in thousands of Roman Catholic churches throughout the world. And, it is claimed, only by the continual offering of this sacrifice that sin can be put away. It is important to realize that the mass is not simply the memorial of the sacrifice of Christ made once on the cross, but is itself a sacrifice for sins. This is what in the eyes of Roman Catholics gives it its power, and makes it central to the worship and theology of the Church of Rome. It also serves to make the laity absolutely dependent on the priesthood for only the priest is empowered to offer this sacrifice for sins.

In this encyclical letter on *The Mystery and Worship of the Holy Eucharist* issued in 1980, Pope John Paul II emphasises again this central concept of the mass, which he considers some priests and laity may have begun to neglect. 'The Eucharist', he states, 'is above all else a sacrifice'. It is today's sacrifice of redemption and, 'the celebrant, as minister of this sacrifice, is the authentic *priest*, performing—in virtue of the specific power of sacred ordination—a true

146

sacrificial act that brings creation back to God'. In view of a tendency by some priests to omit certain words from the liturgy the Pope reminds them that the words of the celebrant, 'pray that my sacrifice and yours may be acceptable to God, the almighty Father' are 'binding, since they express the character of the entire Eucharistic liturgy and the fulness of its divine and ecclesial content'.

This spirited and unequivocal assertion of the traditional teaching of the Roman Catholic Church by the present Pope can leave us in no doubt as to the central concept of the mass both past and present. It is above all things a sacrifice.

The Holy Communion service of the Protestant churches, including of course the Church of England, is not a sacrifice in that sense at all. We have seen how the Reformers were at pains to remove altogether this understanding of the service and to ensure that it was administered 'according to Christ's ordinance'. In careful and measured language they drew a line of distinction between the New Testament teaching on Holy Communion and the Roman doctrine of the mass. They were not indulging in petulance when they described the mass as a 'blasphemous fable' and a 'dangerous deceit'.[4] It was blasphemous, they considered, because it pretended to be a 'propitiatory sacrifice for the sins of the living and the dead', whereas the Bible teaches that there is only one propitiatory sacrifice for sin made once for all by Christ upon the cross. 'My glory', says God, 'I will not give to another'. To take God's glory, that is, that which rightly belongs to him alone, and ascribe it to something or someone else is to commit blasphemy, to dishonour God. That is what the Roman Catholic teaching about the mass does when it takes from Christ the honour of making the one sacrifice for sin and ascribes this power to the actions of the priest in offering the sacrifice of the mass. The language of the Reformers was plain and efficient, and not exaggerated.

The word 'fable' was used because the sacrifice of the mass is not only something that is derogatory to the honour of God, but it is also, they argued, fictitious, something invented and not found in the New Testament. We do not find there any teaching about the efficacy of the sacrifice of the mass. There is teaching about the Communion service, or Lord's Supper, and about the need to receive by faith the benefits of Christ's death made once upon the cross, but nothing about the need to offer further sacrifices for sins. Such teaching is therefore the invention of a later period when the Church began to move away from the Scriptures into error.

Finally, the mass was spoken of as 'a dangerous deceit'. A thing or person is deceitful if it misleads, and claims to be what it is not. The mass misleads with regard to man's salvation; how he may be justified and find peace with God. The Roman Church teaches people that the mass has power to take away their sins, that they will find forgiveness by virtue of the 'work' of attending mass. Masses are said for the souls of those in purgatory that they may be forgiven and their time in its fires shortened. All this is deceitful because it misleads, and diverts attention from the One who alone is able to pardon and justify. It teaches people to trust in a work performed by the church, rather than in the Lord Jesus Christ who is the only Saviour. The mass has no power whatsoever to effect the forgiveness of sins, and because it is represented as having that power it can only properly be described as a 'deceit'. It is of course a 'dangerous deceit' because it misleads men on the fundamental question of their eternal salvation.

Transubstantiation

The Roman Catholic doctrine of transubstantiation, which teaches that when the priest pronounces the words, 'This is my body', and, 'This is my blood'; the bread and the wine before him on the altar become the actual body and blood of Christ in everything but taste, colour and texture, is not an isolated doctrine. It is all of a piece with the tendency in the Church of Rome to put things and persons in the place of God. Thus the Pope becomes God on earth, the priest becomes 'another Christ' and the bread and wine become the real body and blood of Christ.

Transubstantiation is a doctrine to which the Church of

Rome tenaciously clings. Despite superficial changes of language and the simplification of some of the ritual of the mass, at the heart of the matter is still this concept of the power of the priest to make present in the bread and wine on the altar the true, real and substantial body and blood of Christ.[5] Here Rome proves herself to be 'always the same'.

The teaching of transubstantiation is essential to the idea of the sacrifice of the mass. A priest must have something to offer and if he claims to offer the sacrifice of Christ then he must have the actual body and blood of Christ with which to do it. Thus one error grows out of another until you have a whole system of error.

The notion of transubstantiation rests upon a mistaken interpretation of the words of Christ, 'This is my body', etc. When they are placed in their proper context of the Last Supper, in which they were uttered, it is difficult to imagine that they could have been so misinterpreted. Our Lord's usual method of teaching was by parables and figures of speech. When, in the presence of his disciples, he broke the bread and said, 'This is my body', it could not possibly have occurred to them that he meant that the bread was his actual physical body. All the conventions of Hebrew thought, of the acted parable which we find in the Old Testament, would have prevented such a literal understanding. The words could only have been understood symbolically.

It was very much later when men had grown away from Hebrew language and the Hebrew mind that these words and, indeed, the whole of Scripture was given a flat and literalistic interpretation. But that in turn created another problem. If Christ's body were actually present on the altar how could it also be in heaven where Christ had ascended. A body cannot be in two places at once. So a rather contrived and artificial solution was devised by Thomas Aquinas from the philosophy of Aristotle, to this wholly unnecessary question. A body, it was said, has an inner or essential nature which is the same at all times and in all places. It also has certain properties or 'accidents' such as colour, texture and taste which vary in different places. Thomas argued that, when the priest says the words of consecration the whole substance (or essence) of the bread changes into the substance of the body of Christ, while the accidents, (the taste, texture, colour) of the bread remain as they were before, and the accidents of Christ's body remain in the only place where his body is, viz, in heaven.

But the problem was not a real one in the first place. When the Reformation brought a return to the study of the original languages it brought with it a clearer understanding of biblical thought, and the recognition of the real significance of our Lord's words. The doctrine was rejected because a proper understanding of Hebrew thought made such a rationalisation redundant. It was also argued that transubstantiation 'overthrows the nature of a sacrament', because a sacrament is by definition a sign of something, but this teaching turns the sacrament into the very thing it is supposed to signify or stand for.

At the time of the Reformation the doctrine of transubstantiation became the test imposed by the Roman Catholic judges on those Protestants whom they tried for heresy. Did they, or did they not believe that the body and blood of Christ were really, truly and substantially present under the forms of bread and wine after the words of consecration were pronounced? If they did not believe they were burned as heretics. It might seem strange that the conflict between Roman Catholicism and Reformed religion should focus on this point when there are so many differences between them. But it is not, as we have seen, an isolated feature.

All the practices which have flowed from this doctrine of transubstantiation serve only to reveal its deviant nature, such as, solemn adoration, which is the worship of the bread and wine; benediction which is the waving of the Host in blessing over the congregation; the carrying about of the Host in the processions of Corpus Christi; and the locking up of it in the Tabernacle when it is not in use.

Such things must serve only to diminish the spirit of true religion. They are very far removed from meaning of our Lord's words and the purpose for which he instituted the

Holy Communion or Lord's Supper. In that Supper he intended that we should thankfully remember his death on the cross for us, and as we receive the bread and the wine we should by faith receive the benefits of his sacrificial death.

Tradition and Scripture

Few can be unaware of the change which has taken place in recent years in the Roman Catholic Church in relation to the Bible and the laity. The Scriptures are now being circulated and are available in a way in which they were not a short time ago, even in Roman Catholic countries. It is reported that in India the celebration of Bible Sunday is marked with a ceremony of 'enthronement of the Bible in houses' which involves the censing of it and various other acts of homage!

This may suggest to some Protestants that the Church of Rome is becoming more biblically oriented. The new prominence, however, given to the Bible since Vatican II must be understood in terms of the teaching of that council itself, which states, '. . . It is not from sacred Scripture alone that the Church draws her certainty about everything which has been revealed. Therefore both sacred tradition and sacred Scripture are to be accepted and venerated with the same sense of devotion and reverence'. Also, besides adding tradition, or the oral teaching of the church and placing it on the same level as Scripture, the Church of Rome insists that the Bible can only be interpreted by the *magisterium* or teaching office of the church.

Thus the same decree of Vatican II goes on, 'The task of authentically interpreting the word of God, whether written or handed on, has been entrusted exclusively to the living teaching office of the Church'. This of course is vested in the Pope himself.

When these facts are taken into account, it will be seen that the presence and availability of the Bible in the Church of Rome is seriously compromised. The Roman Catholic layman is allowed to use it devotionally, to foster piety, but not to prove doctrine. That is the business of the Pope and the hierachy. By virtue of this teaching office the Word of God is corrupted, something against which the apostle Paul repeatedly warns (2 Corinthians 2:17 and 4:2).

Two examples will show the serious implications of this position and how it brings the Church of Rome under the same condemnation which our Lord pronounced against the Pharisees, when he said that they made the Word of God of none effect through their tradition.

First, let us take those commandments which define our duty to God. The first commandment declares that we must worship God only. The Church of Rome permits the worship of saints, angels and relics. She does so on the basis of a verbal quibble between *latria*, worship which may be paid to God alone, and *dulia*, worship which may be paid to saints.

In the second commandment God forbids the worship of images. The Church of Rome sets aside the second commandment and allows the worship of images. The force of this commandment is evaded by including it under the first and dividing the tenth commandment up into two, in order to make up the number to ten.

God forbids blasphemy in the third commandment. The Church of Rome waives this when she takes the names of God such as 'Holy Father' and ascribes them to the Pope.

In the fourth commandment God commands his day to be kept holy. It is well known that the emphasis in the Church of Rome is upon attending mass, not keeping the day holy.

The concept of man's duty to God is thus thoroughly corrupted by the teaching authority of the Church and the commandments of God are made of none effect through tradition.

Secondly, let us take an example of what the Bible says about Mary and what the Roman Church makes of it. The decree on Mary, of Vatican II states, '. . . her intercession brought about the beginning of miracles by Jesus'. But if we read the story in John 2, that is not how it appears at all. On the contrary Jesus was showing to Mary on that occasion that he was sovereign in the exercise of his power as the Son of God and would tolerate no interference, not even from her, 'Woman, what have I to do with thee? Mine hour is not yet come'.

What is common to these examples is that the Church of Rome has succeeded in making the Bible say the exact opposite to what it is in fact saying. If the teaching office of the Church cannot be trusted here where can it be trusted? Are not the Scriptures twisted and tortured in the interest of the church's dogma and tradition?

There is then a great gulf in principle and practice between the Protestant position of the sole authority and sufficiency of Scripture (as stated in the sixth Article of the Church of England), and that of the Church of Rome. And it seems clear which is more likely to communicate to us the true message of the Bible.

This fundamental difference remains unresolved. There is no indication that Rome intends to change its position. Protestants cannot, and must not, surrender the unique authority and primacy of Scripture. That alone made the Reformation of the Church possible four hundred years ago, and gives hope of its further reformation today. Without it spiritual darkness would quickly overtake Christendom as a whole.

Purgatory

Of all the doctrines invented by the Church of Rome, that of purgatory, with its associated teaching about indulgences, seems to have been one of the most harmful. It is still an integral part of its teaching. The Roman Catholic catechism states that it is 'the place where souls suffer for a time after death on account of their sins'.

Every person, so the Church of Rome teaches, is liable to eternal and temporal punishment for his sins. God, on account of his Son, pardons the eternal punishment for Christians so that they need not go to hell. But even the Christian after death will suffer in purgatory, which is defined as a place where the pain is as intense as that of hell but does not last for all eternity. Thus the temporal punishment due to sins, which God has not forgiven the sinner,

153

has to be worked off by acts of penance in this life, and in a state of suffering and misery hereafter.

A doctrine of this magnitude and importance ought surely to be plainly stated in Scripture, yet a careful study of the Bible reveals no evidence of it. The one or two texts quoted are quite inadequate. Where Paul speaks of being saved 'yet so as by fire' (1 Corinthians 3:12 ff), is a good example, and is also regarded by the Church of Rome as a full proof of its teaching about purgatory. Examination of the passage shows that, first, Paul is not speaking about Christians in general, but teachers in the church, and the nature of the work they do in building up the church, some of which is shoddy and poor workmanship and will not stand the test, but some of it is good and will endure. Secondly, the nature of the test, 'as by fire', refers not to the cleansing of the person, but the testing of the *work* of such teachers in the church, which is a very different thing. Thus the passage has nothing whatever to do with the doctrine of purgatory as taught by the Church of Rome. It is unthinkable that on a matter as important as this our Lord and his apostles would have given the church no clear teaching.

More than this, the Gospel itself makes no distinction like that which the Church of Rome makes between eternal and temporal punishment. There is no suggestion that God reserves a clause relating to temporal punishment when he commands the Gospel of full forgiveness of sins to be preached. What would we think of a government that declared a general amnesty without reserve, but then later, when the offenders came forward, stated that it related only to certain kinds of offences and not to others.

The teaching of the Scriptures on the state of the believer after death contradicts the doctrine of purgatory. To die, says Paul, is 'to depart and be with Christ which is far better' (Philippians 1:23). To have everlasting life, through faith in Christ, means that we 'shall not come into condemnation; but have passed from death to life' (John 5:24).

The doctrine of purgatory inspires fear and binds the laity ever more tightly to the priesthood who claim to be able to release souls from purgatory by the offering of the sacrifice of the mass for the dead, though, strangely, the priest is quite incapable of saying when a soul is released and when such masses should cease.

Associated with this is also the doctrine of indulgences. The church, it is claimed, has the power to remit punishment in purgatory upon the performance of certain pious acts, such as the saying of certain prayers, or visits to holy places.

It is well known that in earlier centuries the Roman Church gained great income from the direct sale of indulgences. Although this iniquitous practice has now been discontinued, the Roman Church still makes huge profits out of indulgences, by the alms which are encouraged when indulgences are sought, and by the sale of rosaries and other articles to which indulgences are attached. We can be sure that if the Church of Rome got rid of its doctrine of purgatory a great part of its wealth would disappear with it.

Article XXII of the Church of England rightly condemns the doctrine of purgatory as 'a fond thing vainly invented and grounded upon no warranty of Scripture, but rather repugnant to the Word of God'. Nothing has happened to change the validity and relevance of those words, and we must be thankful that they speak so plainly and warn so clearly of the danger.

Penance

The sacrament of penance is one of the principal means of grace on the Roman Catholic Church. It is necessary to confess your sins to a priest. The Roman Catholic catechism (revised edition 1971), defines penance as '. . . a sacrament whereby sins, whether mortal or venial, which we have committed after baptism are forgiven'. Thus the Church of Rome teaches that all must ordinarily come to the priest to have sins forgiven. Baptism remits all sins up to the point at which it is received, that of course is usually in infancy. But every sin committed afterwards must be removed by penance, and only a priest can give absolution. Mortal sins are serious sins which cut the soul off from God; venial sins are not so serious and do not have that effect.

It is commonly thought by Protestants, and sometimes Roman Catholic apologists suggest, that contrition, ie. sorrow for sin and the resolve to forsake it, is an essential part of penance. But when the teaching is examined it is seen that contrition is not really demanded. The Roman Catholic catechism goes on to say that the fear of punishment, ie. attrition, is enough for making a confession to a priest. People are thus encouraged to come and confess and receive absolution for mortal as well as venial sins time after time on these terms, with the assurance that to receive such absolution from a priest is the same as receiving it from God.

Recently, a conference of Roman Catholic priests, doctors, social workers and psychiatrists was held to consider the problem of why a quarter of the prison population of Britain is Roman Catholic when Roman Catholics form only one-fifteenth of the total population. One doctor suggested that it was because Roman Catholics were less successful criminals than others, and therefore got caught while the others got away. The conference ought to have considered the harm done by the system of sacramental confession which encourages the offender to confess and receive absolution without the spirit of true contrition.

Confession, which the Roman catechism defines as, 'to accuse ourselves of sins to a priest', was not made compulsory until 1215 AD when the Fourth Lateran Council decreed that it was necessary, 'under pain of mortal sin to confess at least once a year to a priest'. It seems strange that something which was then regarded as necessary was discovered so late. As John Wycliffe put it, 'It seemeth that it is not necessary . . . for Christ, all-knowing, used it not, nor none of his apostles after. And if it were necessary to man Christ would have used it or taught it'. He went on shrewdly to suggest that the real purpose of the decree regarding confession was to make all men subject to the Pope so that he could lead them where he liked. 'Lord, where is freedom of Christ when men be cast in such bondage? Christ made his servants free but Antichrist hath made them bound again. And certainly there is no authority that gave him leave to make men thus enthralled'.

When confession has been made and absolution given there is still penance to be done. This is sometimes no more than saying a few 'Hail Marys', but whatever the penance given the catechism warns that it does, 'not always make full satisfaction for our sins. We should therefore add to it other good works and penances, and try to gain indulgences'. There is always some debt or other to be paid for sin and what is not met in this life is to be met in the life to come in purgatory.

For those familiar with the teaching of the Bible about forgiveness and justification by free grace there can be no greater travesty of the Gospel than this system which has been fabricated by the Church of Rome. The wonder is that people still believe it. But they do and that makes it imperative that we should set forth plainly the true path of justification by faith alone.

Notes

Chapter 1

[1] Charles Davis, *A Question of Conscience*, 69.
[2] Ian Henderson, *Power without Glory*, 12.

Chapter 5

[1] For a fuller treatment of this subject see *The Problem of Catholicism*, Vittorio Subilia.

Chapter 7

[1] *Defence of the True and Catholic Doctrine*, Cranmer's *Works*, Parker Society vol. I, 47.

Chapter 9

[1] *The Pope from Poland*, Ed. John Whale, 190.

Chapter 10

[1] Table Talk, 43.

Appendix

[1] *Mary the Mother of Redemption* 142.
[2] Quoted by J. S. Whale in *The Protestant Tradition*, 253.
[3] *Redemptor Hominis*, 1979, 19.
[4] Article XXXI of the Church of England.
[5] *The Holy Eucharist*, John Paul II, 30.